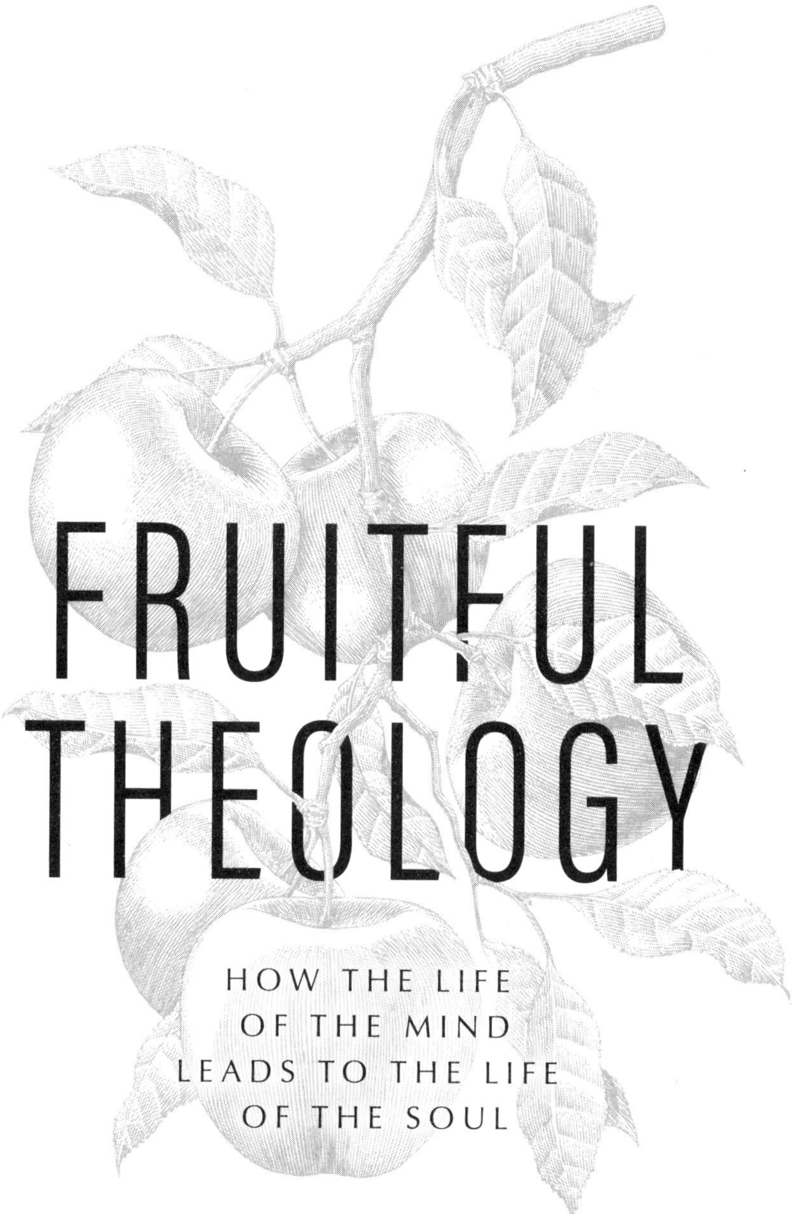

FRUITFUL THEOLOGY

HOW THE LIFE
OF THE MIND
LEADS TO THE LIFE
OF THE SOUL

RONNI KURTZ

B&H
PUBLISHING
NASHVILLE, TENNESSEE

Printed in the United States of America

978-1-0877-5877-0

Printed by B&H Publishing Group
Nashville, Tennessee

Dewey Decimal Classification: 230
Subject Heading: THEOLOGY / GOD / FRUIT OF THE SPIRIT

Cover design by Brian Bobel. Cover image by Channarong Pherngjanda/shutterstock. Author photo by Ronni Kurtz.

1 2 3 4 5 6 • 26 25 24 23 22

To Finley Jane,

May the triune God captivate your mind's eye.
May your contemplation of his glory and grace
bear fruit until your faith is sight.
I love you.

Acknowledgments

Writing a book on the ways theology should sanctify our souls and lead to the fruit of the Spirit is a convicting task. In composing each chapter, specific incidences came to mind in which I failed to demonstrate that particular fruit of the Spirit. Therefore, my first and greatest thanks is to our triune God who saw my helpless estate and did something about it. I thank the Lord that for every instance of my frailty and fickleness he is infinitely faithful; moreover, he didn't reserve his reward but dressed a worm like me in his robes of righteousness in union with his Son.

I wrote much of this book in the summer of 2021. During that summer I spent a lot of time with three authors—Augustine, Gregory of Nazianzus, and Fyodor Dostoevsky. These three authors, each in his own way, added much to this volume. Augustine reminded me that contemplation is among the worthiest of enterprises; Gregory demonstrated that holiness is not optional for the theological task; and Dostoevsky kept beauty and adventure at the front of my mind. A fourth author, John Webster, shows up throughout this short book; and while he's only referenced explicitly in a few places, his thoughts permeate each chapter.

I want to thank the wonderful team at B&H as well. Taylor Combs has been not only a capable editor but also an outstanding friend. His commitment to the glory of God and the good of others is the exact kind of Christian I aim for in this book. If you're wondering what it looks like to live out the words you hold in your hand, use him as a living example. Thanks also to Devin Maddox and Ashley Gorman for believing in the project and giving a young writer the chance to reflect on theological kindness and contemplation. Your investment means more than you know. Also, on the B&H team, thanks to Kim Stanford for compiling the biblical index, Jade Novak and Susan Browne for their creative brilliance and investment in the project.

I'd also like to thank three students, Joel Whitson, Kaden Classen, and Scott Meadows for reading a pre-published version of this book and offering helpful feedback. Thoughtful students are a gift from the Lord and these three have been a gift to me.

Finally, I'd like to thank my family. Like other writing projects, my faithful dad read every word of the manuscript and offered invaluable feedback. He's been in my corner for as long as I have memories, and his support was a key ingredient to finishing the book. Outside of the Lord, my biggest thanks go to my immediate family—my wife and daughter. My wife has been ruthlessly committed to my writing life even though it comes with great sacrifices on her end. She's one of the greatest adventures I'll ever know and one of the deepest loves I'll ever find.

ACKNOWLEDGMENTS

With joy, I dedicate this book to our firstborn, Finley Jane Kurtz. You'll find a few anecdotes about Fin in the volume, and that is largely because I have a hard time thinking of anything other than the gift she is to me. She didn't choose to have a bookish dad, but I'm thankful that even in her young years she's found a treasure in books for herself. I love you Finley Jane; thank you for being my daughter, and thank you for being you.

Contents

Foreword

We suffer today from the idiot notion that there is strong commitment to theological orthodoxy on the one side and a kind and gracious disposition on the other side, and ne'er the twain shall meet. I don't know exactly where it comes from, but you can see the false dichotomy play out on a minute-by-minute basis on social media and week by week in many evangelical churches.

Scratch that. I know exactly where it comes from. It originates with our spiritual enemy, the devil, who likes few things more, I imagine, than to have Christians choose between an ungracious orthodoxy and a convictionless social etiquette and then stake the credibility of the faith on our choice.

For instance, many of us grew up in church cultures where we knew who the "holy" ones were: they were the people not smiling. But is this what true holiness is? Does closeness to Jesus and greater knowledge of the things of God make one dour? If so, of course, who in their right mind would find such a pursuit attractive?

And then many of us have watched as our "kinder, gentler" brethren have gone on to embrace more than needy sinners unreached by the unwilling but to embrace various kinds of sins themselves, compromising in the name of "tolerance" and apostasizing under the label of "deconstruction." Is that what being Christlike is supposed to look like? Turning the mighty oak of the faith once delivered into a tumbleweed blown about by the winds of culture? Jude wrote an epistle warning about this.

But you and I can defy the devil if we want to. And we can defy the spirit of age run rampant even in our churches by rightly obeying the Lord who tells us that real worshippers worship in both spirit *and* truth (John 4:23).

Spirit and truth. Truth and spirit. These are inseparable, contrary to what you might have heard or what you might suspect. We find they meet perfectly, of course, in our sinless Savior, the Man who was (and is) Truth himself but also Life. The Man who refuted bad theology, correcting "conservative" leaders' doctrinal errors one minute and "liberal" leaders' doctrinal errors the next, and also touched the wounded, sympathized with the broken, and condescended (in the good way) to those on the margins of society.

And we can find the spirit and truth of Christ meet in our churches today if we will take seriously the clarion call of a book like this. Ronni Kurtz has done us an absolutely Christian service in painstakingly helping us reorient our vision of holiness to the fruit of the Spirit. For that is what real holiness looks like. It looks like Jesus.

And if we keep our eyes on Jesus, we will see rather straightaway that sound doctrine and the fruit of the Spirit are not mutually exclusive; rather, the former is meant to fuel the latter, and the latter is meant to adorn the former. Ronni understands as both a pastor-theologian and as a Christian that in fact failures on either "side" undermine the credibility of the other. Sound doctrine gives Christlike character its proper shape, its backbone. And Christlike character is how we show our sound doctrine isn't just empty ideology, isn't just for religious show.

I should tell you, also, that Ronni is the right person to write this book, as he is a man who exemplifies this stuff as well as nearly anybody I've ever met in my forty-six years in the church. I have worked closely alongside him at Midwestern Seminary, and our friendship has been one of deep blessing and encouragement to me, primarily because he is one who, as the saying goes, walks what he talks. He is a careful and rigorous thinker after God's thoughts. And he is one of the kindest, gentlest, patient (and so on) men I've ever known. I will just tell you that Ronni is a Jesus-y guy. And if reading a book about theology by a Jesus-y guy is your bag—and, honestly, it ought to be—you've come to the right place.

Jared C. Wilson
Midwestern Baptist Theological Seminary

Chapter One

Why Do the Theologians Rage?

Theology is the study of God and all things in relation to God.[1] When we go about the business of Christian theology, it is God we are after. Alongside the psalmist, the Christian theologian declares, "Who do I have in heaven but you? And I desire nothing on earth but you. My flesh and my heart may fail, but God is the strength of my heart, my portion forever" (Ps. 73:25–26). God is the desire of the theologian's heart; God is the theologian's portion. While theology treats a host of other topics—such as the creation of all things, the redemption of a sinful people, the establishment of the church, the ethics of a Christian life, and even how all things will one day come to a glorious close—it does so first and foremost with God at the center of our thinking. So the study of creation is the study of *God's* handiwork. The study of the church is the study of *God's* people. The study of Christian salvation is the study of *God's* redemption. God is the primary subject of Christian theology, and we put him before all, placing all else in its rightful place, subjected to *him*.

In short, when Christians set their minds toward the deep things of God in the task of theology, we set our gaze on none other than the triune God. Why might a thoroughly God-centered understanding of theology matter for the beginning of this book? Right-sizing God as the subject of Christian theology is of the utmost importance, for doing so will distinguish theology from all other intellectual pursuits. God is more than a set of facts to be examined; he is the one who calls forth the cosmos by the word of his power, and he will be not merely examined but exalted. Whereas other fields might call their students to study propositions and weigh them, Christian theology calls its students to do more than weigh truth claims, they are called to worship.

The goal of theology is a clearer vision of who God is and what he is doing in the world. Given this goal, when we do theology properly, we should not come out the same person. As confusion about God gives way to clarity and we are brought into the truth of the Christian faith, we cannot help but be molded and shaped by it. Throughout the Scriptures, when individuals are brought into the presence of God, they have strong consequences and reactions. Think of Isaiah, for instance, who in chapter 6 of the book bearing his name, "saw the Lord" and the angels who accompanied him. Being in the presence of the holy God caused Isaiah to burst out in desperation and confess his wickedness. Isaiah cries out, "Woe is me for I am ruined because I am a man of unclean lips and live among a people of unclean lips, and because my eyes have seen the King, the LORD of Armies" (Isa. 6:5). Or, moving to the New Testament, think of John, who, in the book of Revelation has a vision of the Lord and records, "When I saw him, I fell at his feet like a dead man" (Rev. 1:17).

The presence of the Lord changes us. When sinners come into contact with his glory and majesty, they will never be the same. While theology should not be confused for the actual presence of the Lord, if doing theology well clarifies for us the person and work of our triune God, it should bring about change within us. As we set out to renew our minds and participate in theological reasoning, we enter into the greatest unfolding drama known to man. In the person of God and the works of God, we witness an eyeful of the beautiful, the good, and the true. In this way, the theological life is a life of adventure. The adventure is an ever-increasing contemplation and comprehension of this beautiful, good, and true God. Therefore, it is the conviction of this book that, as we set out on this adventure of contemplating God and all things in relation to God, we will be transformed. Moreover, the aim of this book is to detail how this transformation should be a transformation into Christlikeness leading to spiritual fruit. To state it plainly, the life of the mind can, and should, lead to the fruit of the Spirit. The result of theology done well should be love, joy, peace, patience, kindness, goodness, faithfulness, gentleness, and self-control (Gal. 5:22).

At this point, you might be tempted to affirm that this sounds right and good for *theologians*, but what has this to do with *me?* If the answer to the question "What is theology?" is "the study of God and all things in relation to God," then the answer to the question, "Who is a theologian?" is simply, "Everyone." We are all theologians, without exception. The perceptive reader may see how these two questions are related. If theology is the study of God, we all—every one of us—have thoughts about God. Even those who claim there is no God are professing a theology. It is no exaggeration or overstatement to say that you, reader, are a theologian. Whether your thoughts of God are elementary, and you are in the beginning stages of forming your convictions, or if theology is an old friend with whom you've spent much time, you are a theologian.

The question of whether you are a theologian has been settled for you. As you think about God and talk of him, you can't help but be a theologian and participate in the task of theology. The more pertinent question, then, is whether you will be a good and faithful theologian. Will you set your mind on things above such that God and his works become both clearer to you and more of a treasure to you? And, in step with this book, will you go about this vital task in such a way that the contemplation of God leads to the manifestation of spiritual fruit in your life?

Another potential complaint at this point in the book might be that your experience with those who practice Christian theology often cannot be described by those virtues that make up the fruit of the Spirit. You might come to this book with many words to describe theologians, but *patient, kind,* and *gentle* might not be among them. This sad reality is the impetus for the work you hold in your hands. Too many people have had a negative experience with either theology or those who wear the title of theologian. At some point along the way, something went wrong with Christian theology. This brings us to our second question: What is the matter with theology today?

What's the Matter with Theology Today?

The simple answer to this question is nothing. Theology is doing just fine, as it has since the opening salvo of mankind. However, there is something off with some of the theological discourse we see taking place in our day. Far from being described by the string of virtues that make up the fruit of the Spirit, much of what is labeled theology today is insecurity and fury disguised as dialogue or thoughtfulness. Even the most cursory scrolling of social media could lead you to the conclusion that you must be angry in order to do theology.

In our day, it is not uncommon to see theology used as a weapon and not as a well of joy. This "weapon" of theology is picked up and used in malicious ways. The prevalence of theology's misuse means you have probably experienced it yourself.

Maybe you've seen theology weaponized as an instrument of division. In this malpractice of theology, Christian truth is used to pit brothers and sisters against one another. Points of doctrine become the boundary lines in which an "us versus them" war plays out. And while there are indeed good and right times to draw lines in the sand, there are also those whose theological boundaries are so ever shrinking that only they and a handful of their followers are seen as those who possess the truth. Discord arises as theology is used to break unity with those fellow image bearers with whom we ought to be marching arm-in-arm toward the promised land.

Maybe you've seen theology weaponized as an instrument of pride. In this malpractice of theology, the accumulation of knowledge amounts to ever-inflating egos, and the search for truth is but a grasp for self-importance. When the streams of arrogance flow from the source of ill-used theology, the goal becomes the applause of our neighbors instead of the good of our neighbors. Instead of bending our intellectual life toward the pursuit of others, we bend others toward the observation of our intellectual capabilities in hopes of praise that ought to be rendered unto the Lord. In this way, theology can become a show; theologians are simply actors on the doctrinal stage hoping their articulation of a theological concept or their turn of phrase may entertain the audience.

Maybe you've seen theology weaponized as a replacement for sanctification and wisdom. There is a temptation to mistake theological clarity and confidence as Christian wisdom. However, a sincere devotion to the Lord is not measured by the memorization of theological lingo and logic. As we shall see in time, God can use theology as a means of sanctification, and it seems he is often pleased to do so. Yet theological intelligence is not a valid reason to downplay or neglect the vital role of emotional intelligence, relational intelligence, cultural intelligence, and the like. Christian sanctification is holistic, and while theology is a necessary ingredient, it is not in itself a sufficient ingredient. The Christian life calls for a multifaceted maturity and wisdom in which we are beckoned to love the Lord with not just all our mind but also all our heart, all our soul, and all our strength (Deut. 6:4–7; Matt. 22:37–40; Mark 12:30–31; Luke 10:27).

These are but a few ways in which theology is abused in our day. As we work through the fruit of the Spirit in the chapters to come, we will witness other misuses of theology as well. But since this book is shaped by the nine virtues that comprise the fruit of the Spirit, it is important to turn here and discuss these glorious traits that should define the Christian theologian.

The Life of the Mind and the Fruit of the Spirit

This book hopes to swim upstream of an understanding of theology in which one must be loud or angry to participate. On the contrary, to repeat, the heart of the book you currently hold, the goal of this work is to show how the life of the mind can actually lead to the life of the soul in the manifestation of the fruit of the Spirit. We will discuss how taking to the glorious task of Christian contemplation should indeed lead to love, joy, peace, patience, kindness, goodness, faithfulness, gentleness, and self-control.

Theology as a means of cultivating Christian virtue, such as the fruit of the Spirit, is not a new idea. Two quick quotations, from two differing time periods, help us see this important point. Hailing from northern Africa, and born in the fourth century, arguably one of the most well-known church fathers is Augustine. This towering figure in church history once stated, "For this is the fullness of our joy, than which there is nothing greater: to enjoy God the Trinity in whose image we have been made."[2]

This is a bold statement from Augustine, yet I believe he is correct. We can go about stoking our joy in uncountable ways—family, food, vocations, vacations, materials, experiences, and so much more. Yet the greatest log in the fire of our joy is the triune God "in whose image we have been made." The enjoyment of the triune God is the purest of all enjoyments. For other joys will come and go. As the grass withers and the flowers fade, lesser joys are here today and gone tomorrow (Isa. 40:8). Yet our God is the same yesterday, today, and forevermore so the joy found in him is an unshakable and pure joy (Heb. 13:8).

However, as Jen Wilkin so wonderfully stated, "The heart cannot love what the mind does not know."[3] If we want to set our hearts free to live in the joy that comes from loving the triune God, we must set our minds on knowing him. Your mind and your affections are closer than you may recognize, and you will see that what you consistently contemplate you will grow to consistently appreciate.

The second quote comes from another well-known theologian in church history. Moving from fourth-century Africa to thirteenth-century Italy, let us hear from the medieval thinker Thomas Aquinas. Aquinas, much in step with the theme of this book, once declared, "The whole of our life bears fruit and comes to achievement in the knowledge of the Trinity."[4] Aquinas, in this quote, shows that there is "fruit" because of our achieving the knowledge of theology. There is a consequence to spending much time at the feet of the Lord in thought: the whole of your life will begin to bear fruit. Contemplating the good, the true, the beautiful—all culminating in our Lord—has the ability to transform hate into love, despair to joy, division to peace, anxiety to patience, animosity to kindness, evil to goodness, disobedience to faithfulness, harshness to gentleness, and indulgence to self-control.

Since the remainder of this book will discuss these glorious virtues and their relationship to the theological life, it is important to dedicate some time in this first chapter to explicit discussion of the fruit of the Spirit. We turn here to Galatians 5 and a brief look at what Paul calls "the fruit of the Spirit" versus "the works of the flesh" especially as they relate to the life of the mind.

The Fruit of the Spirit and the Works of the Flesh

The book of Galatians is a grace-laced dagger that pierces the heart of works of righteousness. Written from a place a deep concern, the apostle Paul pens the letter to the Galatians in distress that they've abandoned the gospel of Jesus Christ. The gospel is the good news that the triune God has done something about our helpless estate in the person and work of Jesus Christ, that sinners may be redeemed back into triune love if they are united to him by faith. It makes sense that Paul is dismayed that the Galatians are forsaking this life-saving message. No other news brings life everlasting like the news of Jesus Christ. Working through the wonder that is justification by faith, the glory of the new covenant over that of the old covenant, the distinguishing marks of the law and the gospel, and more in chapters 1–4, Paul arrives at our chapter—chapter 5.

The opening sentence of Galatians 5 is worth a lifetime of meditation. These six words come together as balm for the weary and restless soul and will have much importance in this book. The chapter begins, "For freedom, Christ set us free" (v. 1). The glorious indicative is followed by a vital imperative, "Stand firm, then, and don't submit again to a yoke of slavery" (v. 1). Christ and his gospel bring freedom, not slavery.

Paul brings up this awe-inspiring truth of the Christian faith to ask the Galatians a vital question, "You were running well. Who prevented you from being persuaded regarding the truth?" (v. 7). Elaborating his question, Paul discusses two ways of living: one, a life well lived; the other, a life in need of reformation. Starting in verse 16, Paul contrasts the fruit of the Spirit and the works of the flesh.

> I say, then, walk by the Spirit and you will certainly not carry out the desire of the flesh. For the flesh desires what is against the Spirit, and the Spirit desires what is against the flesh; these are opposed to each other, so that you don't do what you want. But if you are led by the Spirit, you are not under the law.
>
> Now the works of the flesh are obvious: sexual immorality, moral impurity, promiscuity, idolatry, sorcery, hatreds, strife, jealousy, outbursts of anger, selfish ambitions, dissensions, factions, envy, drunkenness, carousing, and anything similar. I am warning you about these things—as I warned you before—that those who practice such things will not inherit the kingdom of God.
>
> But the fruit of the Spirit is love, joy, peace, patience, kindness, goodness, faithfulness, gentleness, and self-control. The law is not against such things. Now those who belong to Christ Jesus have crucified the flesh with its passions and desires. If we live

> by the Spirit, let us also keep in step with the Spirit. Let us not become conceited, provoking one another, envying one another. (vv. 16–26)

The observant reader might have recognized that there are more vices listed in the "works of the flesh" than there are virtues within the "fruit of the Spirit." Indeed, Paul here lists nine fruit of the Spirit while he lists fifteen works of the flesh with a sixteenth extender, "anything similar." As we will refer back to those virtues that make up the fruit of the Spirit and those vices that make up the work of the flesh, it will prove helpful here to have a chart for comparing and contrasting purposes:

Fruit of the Spirit	Works of the Flesh
Love	Sexual Immorality
Joy	Moral Impurity
Peace	Promiscuity
Patience	Idolatry
Kindness	Sorcery
Goodness	Hatred
Faithfulness	Strife
Gentleness	Jealousy
Self-Control	Outbursts of Anger
	Selfish Ambition
	Dissension

	Factions
	Envy
	Drunkenness
	Carousing
	Anything Similar

We should note here that as we consider these two categories—the fruit of the Spirit and the works of the flesh—there is an asymmetrical percentage of relevance for our conversation about theology. What I mean by this is to simply state that 100 percent of the fruit of the Spirit matter for discussions of doctrine. However, not all the vices that make up the works of the flesh are pertinent for our discussion here, but many are. For example, it is not hard to imagine theology done poorly leading to moral impurity, idolatry, hatred, strife, jealousy, outbursts of anger, selfish ambition, dissension, factions, and envy.

The diagnostic question, then, behind this book is simple: Does the way you think about theology, the way you do theology, and the way you talk about theology typically lead to love, joy, peace, patience, kindness, goodness, faithfulness, gentleness, and self-control? Or does the way you think about theology, the way you do theology, and the way you talk about theology typically lead to moral impurity, idolatry, hatred, strife, jealousy, outbursts of anger, selfish ambition, dissension, factions, and envy? Allow me to make four brief observations about the fruit of the Spirit versus the work of the flesh that might help bring into focus the importance of this diagnostic question.

First, keep in mind the context of verses 19–26. Paul discusses these two lists of virtues and vices in the larger context of Galatians 5, which takes place in the larger context of the book of Galatians as a whole. Recall the opening line of chapter 5: it is for freedom you've been set free. Submitting our thought life to the fruit of the Spirit versus the works of the flesh comes with substantial consequence. For the life of the mind that leads to the fruit of the Spirit is a life of intellectual freedom. We are called to "take every thought captive" (2 Cor. 10:5), and bringing the fruit of the Spirit into conversation with our theological endeavors shows us that either we will obey and take every thought captive, or our thoughts will take us captive. The Christian who bends his or her thoughts toward the fruit of the Spirit is the Christian who lives in freedom, not slavery.

Second, notice that Paul's list here has a singular subject. You might have noticed that it is the "fruit" of the Spirit, not the "fruits" of the Spirit. That is to say, there is no such world in which we are called to cultivate joy and peace but we may forsake self-control, for example. A Christian theology that leads to goodness but not gentleness is incomplete. It is not enough for us to bend our thought life toward a handful of the fruit of the Spirit; we must go after them all. When we bring all of these virtues together, we get a good sampling of *Christian wisdom*. Throughout this book, I will even sometimes use *wisdom* as shorthand for a contemplative life characterized by the fruit of the Spirit.

Third, it is important not to lose the significance of the reality that these are the fruit of "the Spirit." The task we have before us—cultivating a life of the mind that leads to the fruit of the Spirit—is a spiritual task. Reader, it is imperative that you have the Holy Spirit as you seek to bear fruit in and through your mind. Toiling to produce the kind of fruit described in Galatians 5 apart from the help of the Holy Spirit is a fool's errand. In fact, allow me to advise you to consistently pray for the Spirit's guidance as you read this work. Pray that the Lord would allow you the grace to have a thought life and theology that lead to fruitfulness. Pray for joy, pray for peace, pray for kindness, etc. If this is the fruit of the Spirit, enlist the Spirit in your theological journey and allow him to be the great sanctifier he is.

Fourth and finally, return once more to Galatians 5. Just before the passage we quoted at length above (vv. 19–26), Paul describes the destination to which each road will lead. He warns, for those who pursue the works of the flesh, their outcome will be that they "bite and devour one another" and that eventually they "will be consumed by one another" (v. 15).

With much sorrow, we have seen this exact outcome in the theological world. As theologians rage, their zeal is aimed at one another. Instead of linking arms to pursue the Great Commission as fellow laborers, they set out on friendly fire, participating in a made-up war in which no one wins.

Our theology ought not lead to the consumption of our brothers and sisters in Christ. On the contrary, look at what Paul says is the outcome for those who live by the fruit of the Spirit: they will seek to "love your neighbor as yourself" (Gal. 5:14), and we will "carry one another's burdens; in this way you will fulfill the law of Christ" (Gal. 6:2).

To summarize this point by way of stark dichotomy: theology done in the works of the flesh is characterized by strife, fits of anger, dissension, and divisions. Theology done in this way will lead to devouring one another. On the contrary, theology done in the fruit of the Spirit—which is characterized by love, kindness, gentleness, and joy—will lead to bearing one another's burdens and loving our neighbor as ourselves. The drastic difference in outcomes demonstrates the importance of the task at hand: theology used poorly can indeed have sad outcomes, yet theology done well can drive the virtues that make up the fruit of the Spirit deep in our soul such that we become Christians marked by wisdom and stability.

While Paul here has more in mind than just the thought life of Christians, the life of the mind is still a vital arena in the Christian life in which we can seek to love our neighbors as ourselves. If theology is a weapon, then, let it be a weapon of love. May we equip ourselves with this weapon and seek not to consume our brother but to bear his burdens in love.

A Final Word for Our Journey

Bringing this introduction to a close, we look again at its title. Indeed, our day is a day in which many theologians rage. While millions of folks are doing theology faithfully around the world, it is still not a difficult task to find those who do theology in step with the works of the flesh.

For some, the life of the mind is a highway toward *bursts of anger* in which overly confident theologians belittle those who dare disagree with them.

For some, the life of the mind is an avenue that dismisses nuance for novelty and becomes an outpost for *idolatry*.

For some, the life of the mind is an arena of applause that exists for the establishment and satisfaction of *selfish ambition*.

For some, the life of the mind leads to an ever-shrinking list of friends as theologians accuse others of forsaking the truth and consequently bring on *dissension and factions*.

May we move in the opposite direction. In a sea full of anger and division, may we be the type of thinkers who prize stability, wisdom, and kindness. While hot takes get clicks, likes, and retweets, may we care more about beauty, truthfulness, and goodness. May the goal of our theology be the glory of God and the good of others instead of attention and applause. Might our mind's eye be drawn more toward reasonable levelheadedness that pursues theology as a well of joy instead of hot-tempered weaponization that pursues theology as a mere war strategy.

For the remainder of this book, we will press into theology as the study of God and all things in relation to God. In doing so, we will take many twists and turns, examining different theological realities along the way. However, we will not be doing theology for theology's sake. Instead, we will examine points of doctrine, biblical passages, and theological wisdom all with an eye toward the cultivation of spiritual fruit. As we take this journey together, may we experience a *fruitful theology* in which the life of the mind leads to the life of the soul.

Chapter Two

Love

Love permeates the pages of our sacred book. From the beginning clause of Genesis to the concluding glories of Revelation, love plays a major role in this cosmic drama. In love God creates the world out of nothing, and in love he will recreate the world for his glory. In love God justifies the sinner, and in love he sanctifies the saints. From beginning to end, the biblical witness has a thread of love woven throughout.

God Is Love, *Simply Love*

For any account of love to be truly theological, it should start where all theology ought to begin—God himself. We read in 1 John 4:16 three crucial words: "God is love." Though this clause is small, its wonder is anything but.

Notice that the verse does *not* say, "God *has* love." Rather, it says, "God *is* love." This may seem like a minor point, but it is crucial for us to understand the God we worship. When we talk about God's being—who he is—theologians have long used a crucial word in describing God—*simplicity*.

Ironically, the idea of God's simplicity is not necessarily a simple concept. This is because when we hear the word *simple* in our day, our mind is drawn toward understanding this word to mean something like "easy." However, this is not what we mean when we talk about God's simplicity.

In its most basic terms, when Christians discuss God's "simplicity," we are referring to the fact that God is not made up of parts like you and me. For example, I have two arms, a nose, countless hairs, a beating heart, and a few thousand other body parts. All of these "parts" come together to make up my body, but none of them defines me entirely. So, while I hope this does not come to pass, I could lose a body part and still be me. A nine-fingered Ronni is still Ronni.

God is not this way. God is not composed of parts such that he could lose part of him and remain himself. God does not *have* love; God *is* love. Love is not a "part" of God you can cut off or replace; love is essential to God's very being. Moreover, this is true of all of God's attributes. God does not *have* holiness, but God *is* holy. God does not *have* knowledge but *is* all knowing. This is why the theologians of old used to say, "All that is in God is God, and nothing in God is not God." So, when we use the word *simple*, we mean to say that God's essence is not composed of parts but is simple and unified.

Why does this matter? Why start out a chapter on love as a fruit of the Spirit with a teaching like divine simplicity? Because it is crucial for understanding a truly theological account of love and the relationship between the life of the mind and the fruit of the Spirit. For when we enter the presence of God, we enter into the presence of love. Therefore, if we do theology well—which should always bring us to God, lifting our eyes toward him, setting our mind on him—we will be brought into the transforming presence of love.

This point is worth restating as clearly as possible, as it will lay a foundation for a fruitful thought life. Follow with me as I spell out the point in a logical procession:

1. God is love. He does not merely *have* love but simply *is* love.
2. If theology is the study of God and all things in relation to God, theology done well should always point our attention at God and bring us into the presence of God.
3. Therefore, theology done well brings us into the presence of love, as God *is* love.

A doctrine like divine simplicity is not a mere theological abstraction but is crucial in connecting the life of the mind to the fruit of the Spirit. If our theological interests make us appear hateful—consistently sowing division, reading brothers and sisters in the worst of lights, belittling fellow image bearers, inflating our egos, causing us to be hot-tempered—there is a real chance we are not doing *Christian* theology.

As humans, we are influenced by our company. We have a propensity to talk and act like those we spend time with. Theology ought to be one venue through which you spend much time with God, who *is* love. Spending time with this God of love should transform you into a loving disciple.

Now, with the important foundation of divine simplicity under our theological feet and the connection it makes between our mind and our fruit, let's take a closer look at the biblical concept of love and how our theology might make us a loving people.

The Greatest of These Is Love

"Love is a grace of boundless scope."[1] The great British preacher, Charles Haddon Spurgeon, declared this truth from the pulpit of the Metropolitan Tabernacle in 1884. If you attempt to work through the Scriptures from beginning to end with an eye toward all the Bible has to say about love, your conclusion may indeed line up with Spurgeon's. The sheer number of passages that discuss love seems "boundless," let alone the consequences for how Christians ought to live their lives. It is, therefore, nearly impossible to cover all the Scriptures say about love in this entire book, let alone in this brief section. However, it is important to treat a few of these beautiful sections of Scripture with the hopes of getting a biblical view of love before turning to the question of how theology can lead us into a loving life.

Maybe nothing gives away the significant role love plays throughout Scripture more than biblical *superlatives*. You may have heard this word *superlative* before. Perhaps in high school your class voted on senior superlatives and gave out awards for the best smile, cutest couple, or most likely to succeed. These senior superlative awards, while they have an astronomically high fail rate, are handed out to celebrate or recognize the greatest or best characteristics within a graduating class. For something to be "superlative," it must stand out in terms of excellence from others.

In the Scriptures, love receives many of the superlatives. Take, for example, Matthew 22:36–40. In this biblical scene, the Pharisees approach Jesus. One of them, an expert in Old Testament law, tries to put Jesus to the test. Assessing Jesus's understanding of God's law, the Pharisee asks him, "Teacher, which command in the law is the *greatest*?" Don't miss the superlative: the inquiring Pharisee asks Jesus not just which law is important but which is superlative among the rest. *Which is the greatest?*

While you may get varying numbers depending on which Old Testament scholar you consult, most experts in Old Testament law would say there are more than six hundred laws in the old covenant. This Pharisee puts Jesus to task by making him choose one from the bunch to ascribe superlative status.

Jesus answers the inquiring man and gives him not only the greatest commandment but the second as well. Jesus replies, "Love the Lord your God with all your heart, with all your soul, and with all your mind. This is the greatest and most important command." He continues, "The second is like it: Love your neighbor as yourself." Jesus's response puts the importance of love on full display, as both the first and second greatest commandments are commands for Christians to love—first God, then our neighbor.

As if this superlative status was not enough to demonstrate the vital role of love in Christian ethics, Jesus concludes his answer with an astonishing claim, "All the Law and the Prophets depend on these two commands."

Paul makes this same claim just before discussing the fruit of the Spirit: "For the whole law is fulfilled in one statement: Love your neighbor as yourself" (Gal. 5:14). If you've read these popular verses many times, it may be easy to gloss over the wonder within them. Think for a moment about the entirety of the Old Testament story—all the twists and turns of the Israelite people, their centuries-long slavery in Egypt, their wandering in the wilderness, their reception of the commandments, their establishment of a monarchy, their conquests, their entry into the promised land, their prophets, their priests, all their covenant violations. Now imagine that at some point in the story someone shows up and says that all the complexities of the covenant between God and his people can be summarized in this—*love God, love others.*

Love is center stage in a Christian ethic. While other virtues are vital for a holistic vision of Christian sanctification, love is supreme.

First Corinthians 13 has often been dubbed "the love chapter." A few lines from this chapter almost always find their way into wedding services, and for good reason. In 1 Corinthians 13, Paul declares the supremacy and superlative of love. Paul describes four virtues or actions Christians might partake in and shows how each of them, without love, is empty. He writes:

1. If you have speech even as beautiful and elegant as angels, without love you're simply a clanging cymbal.
2. If you have all the wisdom and insight of the Scriptures and theology, without love it will amount to nothing.
3. Even something as grand as faith—if you have the kind of faith that could demand mountains be moved—without love, is worthless.
4. If you have the kind of charitable heart that is willing to give away everything you own but do it without love, you gain nothing.

Paul, then, turns to describe love. Here we see just how remarkable a Christian understanding of love really is. For Paul tells us that love is patient, kind, does not envy, is not boastful, is not arrogant, is not rude, is not self-seeking, is not irritable, does not keep record of wrong, finds no joy in unrighteousness, rejoices in truth, bears all things, believes all things, hopes all things, endures all things, and finally, never ends.

A vision of love that can do and be all these things is a grand vision of love!

Where does theology come in here? You will be sadly disappointed if you try to muster up this kind of love on effort or emotion alone. Often, not even friendly or familial relationships are enough to make us display this kind of love. However, theology can come to our aid, as it grounds our ability to love in something sturdier than our emotions or any kind of earthly relations. When your emotions are fickle and your relationships seem frail, theology can give you the footing needed to spend yourself in love.

Greater Love Has No One Than This

Now that we've established the vitality of love in the Christian life, we turn to consider how our contemplation of God might lead us on the path of love. We've already witnessed the first important connection between theology and our being conformed into a people of love—divine simplicity. As God simply *is* love, and as theology brings us into the presence of God, theology should, therefore, help raise our eyes to the one who is supremely love and supremely loving. In so doing, Christian theology melts away any residual sinful traces of hate that dwell in us.

However, this is not the only way a robust theological life might sanctify God's people into a loving body. In fact, a host of theological realities which, when meditated on, stir up our affections and produce love. We will turn here to the doctrine of the atonement as a primary example.

When reading and interpreting the Scriptures, it is important for us to pay careful attention when the Bible repeats itself. For example, consider the case of John 15:12–17:

> This is my command: Love one another as I have loved you. No one has greater love than this: to lay down his life for his friends. You are my friends if you do what I command you. I do not call you servants anymore, because a servant doesn't know what his master is doing. I have called you friends, because I have made known to you everything I have heard from my Father. You did not choose me, but I chose you. I appointed you to go and produce fruit and that your fruit should remain, so that whatever you ask the Father in my name, he will give you.

This is what I command you:
Love one another.

Jesus repeats himself, almost verbatim, just five verses apart. We shouldn't miss this, as he does it for emphasis.

In John 15:12, Jesus says, "This is my command: Love one another," and just five verses later, in John 15:17, he states again, "This is what I command you: Love one another." This command is central to the Christian way of life. In fact, Jesus elsewhere states that by our love for one another the world will know we belong to him (John 13:34–35). Love for our brothers and sisters is proof of citizenship in the kingdom of God.

Another important aspect of this passage must be considered. Jesus not only gives us the command to "love one another"; he also gives us the model and motivation to do so. Not only are we to "love one another"; we are to "love one another *as he loved us.*" How did Jesus love us? The answer to this important question comes in the next line and becomes our model and motivation for true love—Jesus laid his life down for us (15:13).

The death of this carpenter from Nazareth changed the world, but not just the world in general; the death of this carpenter changed *my* world. In the death of Jesus, I receive the beautifully gruesome display and example of true love, and as I behold his shed blood on my behalf, my life is indelibly changed. For the scene of Jesus's death is not the scene of just another Middle Eastern man passing away. No, the death of *this* man changed everything; the death of *this* man is a scene of cosmic consequence to which generations of people will cling for the hope of salvation.

Faith Seeking Understanding

While this scene is already awe inducing, this is where theology can fan the flame of our affections. The great medieval theologian Anselm of Canterbury famously described theology as the task of "faith seeking understanding."[2] The sequence of these three words is significant, and we ought not reverse them. Theology is *faith* seeking *understanding,* not *understanding* seeking *faith.*

We are to take up the theological task from a posture of faith and not suspicion. We do not cling to Jesus by knowledge but by faith. Intellect has never saved a soul, but faith has brought countless individuals into the kingdom of heaven. Once the Spirit has given us the gift of faith, we are free to pursue a better understanding of that in which we have faith. Faith is the entry prerequisite into the arena of theology.

Faith seeking understanding is important in discussions about the death of Jesus. As we explore the doctrine of the atonement and how it might lead us to love, we should point out that we need not know every detail and nuance of the atonement to appreciate it. However, once we have simple faith in the life-altering news of Jesus's death, we can then press in a bit further intellectually. As we do, we will find wonder upon wonder.

Theology, in this case, helps bring what is unclear into focus. As the details of Jesus's death come into focus, we see just how consequential Good Friday was and is in the life of believers. If the atonement is the model and motivation for Christian love, and theology helps bring the atonement into clarity, theology can therefore help us lay hold of our model and motivation for love. Our theology, then, ought to move us to being a people increasingly marked by love.

As we saw above in John 15, the Scriptures tell us the greatest act of love is laying your life down for another: "No one has greater love than this: to lay down his life for his friends" (John 15:13). However, while there are heroic tales of those laying down their life for those they love, Jesus goes a step further—and this is an important step. Jesus doesn't just lay his life down for his friends but also for his enemies. Romans 5 tells us, "God proves his own love for us in that while we were still sinners, Christ died for us" (v. 8). Ephesians 2 tells us, "God, who is rich in mercy, because of his great love that he had for us, made us alive with Christ even though we were dead in trespasses" (v. 4–5).

This moment in the drama of God's people—Jesus Christ laying down his life for a people who were his enemy—is a treasure trove of theological amazement and wonder. You could spend the rest of your days plumbing the depths of beauty contained in the death of Christ, and you would run out of time.

The atonement is the doctrine of a God who has everything and needs nothing laying down his life for people who have nothing and need everything.

While not unlocking every nuance, theology can help our faith seek understanding. It's an opportunity to marvel at the atonement and allow the grace of Christ's crucifixion to lead our souls to love. Just think about the simple phrase *Christ died for you*. While this four-word clause is already beautiful in the truth it contains, if we enlist theology to aid our understanding, it becomes all the more remarkable.

Christ. When we say *Christ* died for you, the primary subject is Christ himself. Theology helps us keep in mind who is at the center of it all. This Christ is the King of kings, the one through whom, for whom, and to whom all things were made (Col. 1:16; Heb. 2:10). Christ is the ever supreme and ever constant Creator of the cosmos before whom every knee will bow and every tongue confess (Isa. 45:23; Rom. 14:11; Phil. 2:10–11). He is the holy one who, while he was in the form of God, did not count equality with God a thing to be grasped and emptied himself by taking on the form of a servant (Phil. 2:6–7). He is the infinite who became an infant, as Spurgeon said.[3] Christ lived a perfect life and grew in obedience, even obedience to the point of death. This man from Nazareth never spoke a wrong word, never thought an ill thought, never performed a wrong action. He is ever faithful and true.

The creeds and confessions of old tell us that Christ is the eternally begotten, only Son of the Father, who is light from light and true God from true God.[4] He is the one who simultaneously lay in the manger and held the universe together by the word of his power, the one who simultaneously had his flesh pierced to a Roman cross while he was upholding the life of the men who drove the stakes into his hands. He is the one who conquered death in his death and in victory rose to the right hand of the Father. Finally, he is the one who will one day come again as the Faithful and True to judge the living and the dead and to once and for all win his blood-bought bride, who will reign with him forever.

Died. When we say Christ *died* for you, the second word is both mysterious and marvelous. It is mysterious, as Jesus Christ is the second person of the Trinity. It is not the case that Christ merely has enough attributes of God to be considered God. No, on the contrary, Jesus is the same essence as the Father and *is* God. Therefore, in his divine essence, it is impossible for this one to die. However, as Christ assumed human flesh to live the life we failed to live, he completely died a horrible traitor's death by virtue of his human nature.

While it is mysterious, it is also marvelous. For in the death of this man, Jesus Christ the righteous, you and I can find our hope of eternal life. In the spilled blood of this man, we find a fountain of life. Because he died in payment for our sins and now lives as our high priest, we can be bold enough to approach the Father in prayer, confessing our shortcomings and our needs.

Even though he was perfect in thought, deed, and word, which made him deserving of the reward of heaven, he died the death we deserve. His life was the life we ought to have lived, and his death is the death we ought to have suffered. The Christian gospel tells of a great exchange in which Jesus takes on our sin and we take on his righteousness. That day when Jesus died on Mount Calvary is both mysterious and marvelous.

For you. When we say Christ died *for you,* we declare that this glorious act of atonement had an undeserved benefactor. While Romans 6:23 tells us that the wages of sin is death—and we all are sinners—Christ tasted the bitter death on your behalf.

Remember, Christ died for us *while we were still sinners.* This is marvelous news for those who could have never become friends of Christ on our own power! Christ's death taking place while we were enemies of God means that Christ did not die for some future version of you that has your problems fixed or sin managed. Christ did not die for what he hoped you would become. No, Christ died *for you,* the actual *you.* The *you* that stumbles more than you'd like to admit, the *you* that has the one besetting sin you cannot quite get rid of, the *you* that falls for self-hatred, or lust, or pride, or fear, or whatever else may lurk at your door.

Christ died *for you.*

Theology can be our tour guide on the search for beauty, as we've seen in the simple yet profound sentence *Christ died for you.* While we do not necessarily need theology to appreciate the atonement as a life-changing event, theology can be a vehicle that takes us on the journey of faith seeking understanding, helping our hearts be transformed by what our mind contemplates.

So, then, we return once again to our first fruit of the Spirit—love. If the greatest love is to lay down one's life for another, then you and I as Christians know the greatest love that ever was—the love of Christ for his bride. If the greatest commandment is to love God with all our strength and soul and love our neighbors as ourselves, theology aids our faithfulness to the great commandment by giving us an avenue to explore our model and motivation for loving others—the death of Christ on our behalf.

The atonement for our sins found in Jesus's death is but one theological reality that should motivate the Christian to love. While we could spend the rest of this book exploring alternative theological concepts that might move us to love God and our neighbor, we will instead let the atonement be our test case and now move to discuss what a theologically fueled love might look like in our day-to-day lives.

Theologically Fueled Three-Directional Love

God is love. Christ demonstrated God's love by laying down his life for us while we were still his enemies. Theology helps faith become understanding as we explore the details of this life-giving love in the doctrine of the atonement, which, as we study it, helps us be increasingly transformed into a loving people. In this final section of the chapter, we turn to a consideration of what a theologically fueled love actually looks like. The combination of the biblical testimony and Christian wisdom seems to point toward a three-directional love—love of God, love of others, and a healthy love of self.

Love of God

First John 4:19 tells us that the direction of our love for God and God's love for us has a clear pattern: "We love because he first loved us." In fact, the Scriptures teach us that God loved us even before the foundation of the world (Rom. 9:11; Eph. 1:4–6). God's love for us enables our love for God.

What's more, in the contemplation of how God displayed his love for us, we might find the fuel needed to love God in return. It is the preeminent joy and responsibility of Christians to love God. As the greatest of all the commandments, we set our affections Godward, and our pilgrimage takes us from one degree of love to another for this God who has ransomed our wayward souls.

Love of Others

In his book *The Four Loves,* C. S. Lewis depicts the danger of loving another and the vulnerability that comes with it.

> To love at all is to be vulnerable. Love anything and your heart will be wrung and possibly broken. If you want to make sure of keeping it intact you must give it to no one, not even an animal. Wrap it carefully

> round with hobbies and little luxuries; avoid all entanglements. Lock it up safe in the casket or coffin of your selfishness. But in that casket, safe, dark, motionless, airless, it will change. It will not be broken; it will become unbreakable, impenetrable, irredeemable. To love is to be vulnerable.[5]

Lewis is of course correct. To love our neighbor is a dangerous endeavor. Loving our neighbor often involves a necessary inconvenience, as we lay down ourselves for the good of our neighbor. It is often easier to love the idea of "mankind" without bothering to love our actual fellow man. Yet the chorus of "one another" commands in the New Testament—to love one another, look after one another, mourn with one another, bear one another's burdens, etc.—demands that we actually step into the messy particularities of our neighbors' lives.

While entering into the joys and burdens of our neighbors might be exhausting work, it is worthy work. Theology can help us. As we set our minds on how the Lord loves us wayward sinners, we find more than enough impetus to get out and love our neighbors. When our mind's eye catches a gaze at just how great God's love is for us, love will move us. Love will move Christians to adopt the fatherless, to feed the hungry, to nurse the sick, to pursue the lost, to insist on kindness, and to count our neighbor as more important than ourselves.

Love of Self

I have a gravitational pull toward self-criticism and self-hatred. I've spent hours in prayer and in counseling rooms to work against the intense inward pull toward critical self-analysis, but it still resides within me. I know I'm not alone in this fight against the flesh. As a pastor, I've heard of countless Christians who struggle with self-worth and a healthy sense of self-love.

Of course, in our world it's easy to take a nuanced and careful understanding of love for oneself and let it devolve into selfishness or self-centeredness. That error of pride is not what we are after here. Instead, there is a place in Christian wisdom for a healthy measure of love for yourself, and theology might be one tool we can use to pursue this form of Christian maturity.

God created all things and called them "good," but when God created man and woman, he called them "very good" (Gen. 1:31). Humans are made in the image of God, and by virtue of our Creator, there is something innately *good* about us. While sin has tarnished all we see and experience, and while our transgressions have taken much from us, our sin cannot take away our status as those who bear the image of our Creator. Moreover, the command to "love our neighbor as ourselves" implies that we have a healthy measure of self-love. Christians can grab hold of theology to gain a right-sized view of *who they are*—which is one riddled with sin and corruption but *also* one treasured and redeemed by God. In the tension of life as a sinner and a saint, there is a place for theologically informed love of self.

Love, the Leading Virtue

It was by no mistake that love leads the list of virtues that make up the fruit of the Spirit in Galatians 5. Love is central to both the great commandment and the Great Commission. In that one word—*love*—we see the fulfillment of the law. So then, while this book will aim to demonstrate how theology can lead to *all* the fruit of the Spirit, we are right to prioritize love and to give it the longest chapter in this book.

In Colossians 3, Paul exhorts us to "put on" compassion, kindness, humility, gentleness, and patience. However, just one sentence later he writes, "Above all, put on love" (v. 14). Theology expands our minds; may it also enflame our hearts toward love. As Christians who love truth, may the life of the mind make its way into the life of our soul, helping us "put on love" in all we do.

Chapter Three

Joy

"What is our purpose on earth? Why are we here?"

This question about purpose has lingered on the lips of curious men and women for generations. One of the most famous answers to this ever-important question—and the answer I hold to—came in the 1640s, when the writers of the Westminster Shorter Catechism made this the first question they treated. In the catechism—which is simply a list of questions and answers often used for children, new converts, and adult discipleship—the authors asked, "What is the chief end of man?" Their answer is etched into the memory of countless souls over the last four centuries, including my own.

"Man's chief end is to glorify God and enjoy him forever."

That is what you were made for—to glorify God and to enjoy God. Your days, as many as the Lord might give you, should be filled with those two great pursuits. If even the moments in which you hold this book you feel a longing in your soul for purpose, you might just find it in a lifelong endeavor to enjoy God.

Furthermore, I think John Piper was onto something when he made his one-word tweak to the famous answer. In tweaking *"and"* to *"by,"* Piper shows not only the chief end of man but the chief method to get to the end: the chief end of man is to glorify God *by* enjoying him forever.[1]

One significant way we glorify the Lord among all the peoples of the world is by enjoying him as the source of greatest pleasure to be found. As the psalmist declares, "You reveal the path of life to me; in your presence is abundant joy; at your right hand are eternal pleasures" (Ps. 16:11). In this psalm and in many other portions of Scripture, we are confronted with the reality that if we are after joy, our aim ought to be the presence of God. Consequently, if theology is "the study of God and all things in relation to God," joy being found in the presence of God is good news. For our efforts in theology should bring us into the presence of God, which is the supreme location of "the fullness of joy."

Finding how to enter into the "fullness of joy" is an important discipline in the Christian life. Proverbs tells us that "a joyful heart is good medicine, but a broken spirit dries up the bones" (Prov. 17:22). The regular rhythms of the Christian ought to be riddled with joy; we are to have joy on our minds even as we arise each morning. For today "is the day the LORD has made; let's rejoice and be glad in it" (Ps. 118:24). Indeed, in the Lord, "my heart is glad and my whole being rejoices" (Ps. 16:9). Even our repentance is a repentance into joy. Like David, when we move from wickedness to righteousness, we ought to beseech the Lord to "restore the joy of your salvation to me" (Ps. 51:12).

As these verses show, Christians ought to be well acquainted with joy. If these verses—and those that follow in this chapter—are not enough to demonstrate the vital place of joy in the Christian life, notice that we are even *commanded* to have joy: "Rejoice in the Lord always. I will say it again: Rejoice!" (Phil. 4:4). Joy is not negotiable in the Christian life; it permeates our rhythms, our personalities, our words, our actions, and just about all we are. We are to be a joyful people.

Joy Needs Roots

Given the important place of joy in the Christian life, it is vital that our joy be not equated with merely "the absence of sorrow" or "the presence of a smile."[2] Indeed, theology will not save you from sorrow; it does not have that power. Yet the good news is that Christian joy speaks a better word than a mere absence of sorrow. Joy is deeper than the lack of sadness.

If joy is to be all it is meant to be, joy needs roots. Here theology can really aid the Christians pursuit of joy—finding a sure soil in which to root our joy, such that the bedrock of our joy might not be fickle or frail.

C. S. Lewis once commented that the enjoyment folks often look for in "books of devotion," he actually finds in "books of theology." Lewis writes:

> Nor would I admit any sharp division between the two kinds of book. For my own part, I tend to find the doctrinal books often more helpful in devotion than the devotional books, and I rather suspect that the same experience may await many others. I believe that many who find that "nothing happens" when they sit down, or kneel down, to a book of devotion, would find that the heart sings unbidden while they are working their way through a tough bit of theology with a pipe in their teeth and a pencil in their hand.[3]

Lewis's point here is important for us, for he is making the astute observation that joy is to be found in theology, even a "tough bit of theology," which will need tending to with careful attention.

Those who find joy in theology have often learned the important lesson that joy needs roots. Yet the obstacles to joy are numerous in our world. Like never-ceasing tides rolling up against the beach, waves of sorrow can follow, one after another, and push against us in ways that make victory over anger, sorrow, resentment, bitterness, and the like seem like an impossible destination. If your joy has shallow roots, it will snap. The headwind blowing against joy is far too strong to find it in that which is fleeting and in flux. We are wise, instead, to find ways to root our joy—to make it sturdy against whatever headwinds may come against it. While theology is not a sufficient condition for joy, it is nevertheless a necessary condition for abundant joy.

Theology Leads to Joy

If joy needs roots, theology is one tool the planter may use to make sure the Christian's delight is firmly planted. Given that the journey of theology is a lifelong endeavor, we are sure to find countless ways our contemplation of God might lead to our enjoyment of God. Here are four ways I have personally seen the glorious work of thinking about God lead to a greater enjoyment of God: (1) being confronted by the good, the beautiful, and the true; (2) contemplating what we deserve compared to what we get in Christ; (3) seeing confusion give way to clarity; and (4) the deep dependence developed in relying on the Lord in Christian theology.

Confronting the Good, the True, and the Beautiful

Theologians, philosophers, and humanitarians in general have long talked about what has come to be known as "the transcendentals." While there is disagreement about the origin of this idea, or even how many "transcendentals" exist, the idea is fairly simple—as humans, we long for that which is good, that which is beautiful, and that which is true.

Often in the face of the good, the beautiful, and the true, we are led to worship or action. Maybe you've experienced a deep longing for justice and a heartache when someone or something is ill treated. Your longing for justice is likely rooted in your longing for the good.

If you've ever experienced a truly breathtaking view of nature, like the Grand Canyon in Arizona or the Fjaðrárgljúfur Canyon in Iceland, you might have felt a nearly inexplicable sense of appreciation of the majesty and beauty of earth. Or maybe you have experienced the beauty of a piece of art—perhaps in a great novel like *The Brothers Karamazov* or *Jane Eyre*. The eyeful of the gaping canyon or the development of a grand novel are but a few examples of our deep longing for beauty.

Finally, as humans, we long for the truth. There is a reason we are wired to be offended when we have been on the receiving end of a lie. The desire for truth is engrained in us, and we will even go to seemingly absurd lengths to obtain the truth. Simply put, we as humans desire the good, the beautiful, and the true.

It is vital we recall the doctrine of divine simplicity once again. For God does not merely *have* goodness, beauty, and truth. Rather, God *is* good; God *is* beauty; God *is* truth. Therefore, our adventuring into theology is nothing short of being confronted with ultimate goodness, ultimate truth, and ultimate beauty. Our experience of God, even through theology, as the good, the beautiful, and the true, will in time satisfy our deepest longings in life for something grander than ourselves

At this point we see how important it is to keep our definition of theology in hand. For if theology is the study of God and all things in relation to God, we see that God is the goal of theology. In God we get the true, the beautiful, and the good—not in theology in and of itself. However, as theology leads us into contemplation of God and all things in relation to God, it is a precious tool in the hands of the Christian. The more time we spend confronted with goodness, truth, and beauty, the more joyful we will be.

What We Are Compared to What We Deserve

Not only does theology lead us into the presence of the good, the true, and the beautiful, but particular elements of theology are also themselves true, good, and beautiful. Take, for example, the unfolding drama of the gospel. In the gospel we hear of a disobedient people—the Israelites—and their inability to follow the law God set forth for them. This God promised the Israelites that if they followed his law, he would be their God and they would be his people. However, if they disobeyed the law, it would lead to death and destruction. As the story unfolds, we see that only one party is able to keep its end of the deal. While people are unable to obey the law, God remains their God. In fact, he is so eager to love these rebellious people that he sends his own Son, the second person of the Trinity, to live the life of obedience they should have lived. Instead of claiming the reward for his perfect life, Jesus gives the reward to God's rebellious people—and not only to them but to all the peoples of the world. In exchange, he takes on the punishment they deserved due to their wickedness and disobedience to God's law.

In this "great exchange" in which Jesus takes our wickedness and gives us his righteousness, we are confronted with a staggering comparison. When we compare what we *deserve* in our sin to what we *received* in Christ, it brings us into a place of eternal joy. In our sin we deserve the death and destruction promised by God for disobedience. Yet in Christ we receive every spiritual blessing. We are adopted as sons through Jesus Christ such that now we can run to the Father with "Abba, Father" on our lips, knowing we will never be turned away (Eph. 1:3; Rom. 8:15). The Son of God was despised so that those who should have been despised became sons of God.

Considering the gospel theologically helps us root our joy in a story where we receive the reward of Christ because he received the punishment of our sin. There is fuel enough in this news for a lifetime of joy.

Confusion Gives Way to Clarity

Of our four ways in which theology might lead to joy, this may be the simplest. Theology is a tool that leads us into a greater view of who God is and what he is doing in the world. This tool aids in our move from confusion to clarity.

Theology is one of the many tools Christians can pick up in deciphering what is going on around them and what their place in this unfolding story might be. It gives us handles to hold as we work to make sense of the world and what God is up to in our day and in days past.

Moreover, theology is a vital tool to have as we approach the Scriptures. You may have heard that you should not impose your theology on the Bible and instead should come to the Scriptures as a blank slate ready to be written upon. While this is a noble notion, it is nevertheless a mistaken one. Instead, we ought to approach the Bible with our theology in hand and use it to aid us in making sense of all the glory our sacred book contains. Without theology, there is a danger in the Bible's remaining a book of loosely related material that merely teaches morality. With Christian theology at our side, we can see the Scriptures as a unified story, making a unified point, with a unified end—all of which point toward the glory of our triune God.

Theology is a great aid in assisting the Christian's movement from confusion to clarity. As the fog lifts and our mind's eye catches a glimpse of our God and his glorious work, the result will be a deep and abiding joy.

Intellectual Dependence on God

During my freshman year of college, I was presented with a theological conundrum. The question lodged itself in my mind and haunted me. I thought of it while doing normal, everyday tasks and chores. While we will talk about this season of my life more in-depth in chapter 5, it is helpful to illustrate our point here as well.

The problem was on the forefront of my mind when I went to bed at night and when I woke up. Likely the severity of my preoccupation with this question was not due to the difficulty of the problem but more due to the fact that I was so new to theology. This was the first time a theological problem captivated my curiosity.

What transpired in the following weeks was an adamant and zealous hunt for truth. I read and reread numerous passages, listened to sermons, asked those wiser than myself, watched debates online, read old and new books, and more. However, one other action I took during this theological hunt was prayer. I *begged* God to reveal the truth to me and to give me wisdom.

Eventually the theological confusion gave way to clarity, and I started to understand the intellectual problem a little better. While I got over the theological debate happening in my mind, I never got over how the theological debate made me *feel*—dependent on God.

While theological confusion can cause many Christians to doubt their faith, it does not have to be this way. In fact, theological confusion could (and should) actually lead us to the feet of God, earnestly requesting the wisdom needed to make theological decisions with faithfulness and fidelity. That intellectual crisis in my freshman year caused me to rely on God for my mind, and I will forever be grateful. What I found that year, and every year since then, is that there is a joy to be had in the dependence on God needed to do theology well as a Christian.

If it is God we are after in theology, then it is God we must depend on, and depending on this God will lead to much joy.

Two Consequences of a Theologically Rooted Joy

Unshakable Joy

It is not hyperbole to suggest that rooting your joy in truth is life changing. A joy rooted in who God is and what he is doing will find ways to express itself in most every area of your life. Maybe you have been around the kind of Christian who exudes stability and wisdom. Maybe you have seen the kind of Christian who, while the world seems to be in chaos around them and panic is a normal part of others' operating rhythms, seems to be steady—not fluctuating with the cultural winds. We can only become this kind of stable and wise Christian when our joy is rooted in something more permanent than our feelings, the news headlines, how our political party is doing, our bank accounts, etc.

One vital ingredient in Christian wisdom and stability is placing our joy in the secure confines of God. Given that God is immutable, meaning that he is unchanging in his plans, parts, passions, potentiality, and process, and that he does not even possess the possibility of change, if we root our joy in him, it will be similarly unshakable.[4]

How We Treat Those We Disagree With

The burden of this chapter is to show that theology should be a deep well of joy. As we encounter God *as he really is* and witness the glory of his work in the world, the residual effects of anger and sorrow can melt away, and joy might spring up in their stead. However, many Christians have not experienced theology as such. Instead, scores of believers have seen themselves, or those they care about, pick up theology and become increasingly angry or divisive. As truth is divorced from grace, some have found ways to weaponize theology as a tool for worldview wars and church debates. Yet there is a major difference between those who see theology's primary usefulness as a war tactic and those who view theology as a well of joy.

If we try to interpret the former group in their best light, we could at least say that this group cares so much about truth that they are eager to see their fellow brothers and sisters put down falsehood and pick up truth. However, I would like to postulate that theology as joy is in fact more persuasive as a means of theological and worldview conversion than theology as a weapon.

When we see theology as a weapon or war tactic, we view those who disagree with us as intellectual rivals who must be overcome. This can often be taken to extreme measures, as people treat their "theological opponents" horribly by mocking and publicly deriding them. When we see theology primarily as a war tactic, what ensues is often belittling, name-calling, mischaracterization, oversimplification, and a posture that seeks to "win the argument" regardless of what it means for the person on the other side of the theological aisle (or those watching the debate unfold).

On the contrary, if we view theology as joy, we can see those we disagree with as fellow pilgrims on the journey of contemplating God and warn them that there is abounding joy to be had in the truth. We can insist that they are leaving joy on the field and that walking in the truth will bring a more deeply rooted gladness of their soul than partaking in falsehood. Those who partake in theology as joy instead of war need not feel threatened when others disagree with them. Instead, they are free to feel compassionate and long for their interlocutor to feel the delight that comes with truth. Instead of cutting others down *with* truth, we ought to build those we disagree with up *in* truth.

Come to the Well

After winning his third Super Bowl, Tom Brady sat down with *60 Minutes* for an extended interview about the mindset he carries into competitive athletics. The interview was a raw look at how arguably the greatest football player of all time thinks about success and what he has left to accomplish in his career. At one point in the intimate interview, Brady revealed that while he has tasted great success, he was not close to satisfied with what he had accomplished with his days. In a now oft-quoted portion of the interview, Tom Brady told the interviewer:

> Man, I'm making more money now than I thought I could ever make playing football. . . . Why do I have three Super Bowl rings, and still think there is something greater out there for me? . . . Maybe a lot of people would say, "Hey, man, this is what it is." I reached my goal, my dream, my life. Me, I think, God, *it's got to be more than this.*[5]

We have heard from C. S. Lewis once in this chapter, and it could prove helpful to return to him once more in bringing this chapter to a close. In his book *Mere Christianity,* Lewis writes about that feeling Brady described in his interview and that feeling which is all too familiar for most of us—longing. Lewis writes about that nagging feeling captured in the exasperated, "There has *got* to be more than *this.*"

Lewis writes, "If I find in myself a desire which no experience in this world can satisfy, the most probable explanation is that I was made for another world." He continues, "If none of my earthly pleasures satisfy it, that does not prove that the universe is a fraud. Probably earthly pleasures were never meant to satisfy it, but only to arouse it, to suggest the real thing."[6]

While most of us will never win professional football games or write world-renowned books, just about all of us can relate to the feeling that what I'm experiencing in my day-to-day life *cannot be all there is to this life.* Lewis is right in suggesting that this feeling of unfulfillment should instruct us that this life is not all there is. While being unfulfilled can be a joy destroyer, raising our gaze from the limits of this life can be fulfilling beyond measure.

It is the triune God of the universe that our hearts are longing for in all our feelings of unfulfillment. There is a well in which our soul needs to drink, and that well does not contain waters found in this world. Theology will not be enough to fulfill all your deepest longings. Trying to use theology to do so will indeed be an abuse of theology as we force it to be more than it has the power to be. However, as theology raises our eyes on the Lord of all and as theology brings us into the presence of our Creator, it is a well of joy we should visit often.

Allow me to bring this chapter to a close by offering a challenge: come to the well. Come to the deep well of joy that is Christian theology and allow your thoughts to carry you up and out to something bigger than yourself. The well of theology is deep, and in it is deep joy. Come drink from the waters that are the doctrine of the Trinity, the mighty movement of creation, the teachings of Christ's life and death, the wonder that is redemption, the beauty of the church, the glories of the last things, and so much more.

Theology is a deep well of joy. The fresh springs of God's truth that flow into this well are variegated and beautiful. Come and drink from the well of theology as one way to satisfy the unfulfilled longings of your soul. While Christian theology does not have the necessary conditions to satisfy those deep longings in itself, it might just point you to the one who does—our great God.

Chapter Four

Peace

We have a growing sickness in our day. This sickness is contagious, and it has found a way to seep into even the smallest of our cultural corners. Our sickness is division and discord. We have been infected with disunity, and the sickness has found its way into the church.

Fellow image bearers, our neighbors and families, are being separated into ever-fracturing tribes, and the "us versus them" mentality has developed a gravitational pull in our cultural moment. What is more, the screens in our homes and in our pockets are saturated with talking heads telling us that our problems and worries are the product of those we disagree with. Conglomerate social media corporations are spending billions of dollars to make sure you stay in a state of outrage because outrage drives attention, and attention drives dollars. All you need to disdain your neighbor is Internet access.

The church is not safe from this growing disease of division. Your news feeds and social feeds systematically offer you a steady diet of self-affirming articles that state *this* election or *this* theological disagreement is the one that will make or break the church. When stakes are constantly elevated to do-or-die levels, we can justify any tactic that gives "our side" an edge in the war of thought. Denominations, churches, and church members who once enjoyed deep unity are finding themselves growing apart. Those we used to march with arm in arm are now at arm's length, and we view those we're called to love with greater and greater suspicion. It seems that our culture has never been more eager to draw lines in the sand and never been slower to listen in love. As our tribalism grows, our ability to nuance diminishes, and it becomes increasingly difficult to pursue levelheaded reasoning and Christian wisdom.

We are watching the unfolding in our day of Paul's warning in Galatians 5:15, "But if you bite and devour one another, watch out, or you will be consumed by one another." Not only do we consume one another, but we even dare boast in our consumption. On repeat are video clips of our favorite politician or shock-jock cultural commentator "owning" their opponents. The poison that is divisive exaggeration, hyperbole, straw-manning, and intellectual suspicion has found a home on the tongues of some of our most popular theologians as well. Instead of living out their calling as dispensers of Christian wisdom who seek to interject the beautiful, the good, and the true into our cultural rhythms and conversations, some theologians are gaining a following on the back of a secular playbook that calls for demeaning any who dare disagree.

Into this wildfire of devouring one another and rising division, Paul's command in Romans 12 pierces through the marrow of our cultural plight and demands better of us. Paul instructs the church at Rome, "Live in harmony with one another. Do not be proud; instead, associate with the humble. Do not be wise in your own estimation. Do not repay anyone evil for evil. Give careful thought to do what is honorable in everyone's eyes. *If possible, as far as it depends on you, live at peace with everyone*" (12:16–18, emphasis added).

The command to "live at peace with everyone" is a mighty command that demands much of us. In fact, it is a command that necessitates more than theology can offer on its own. However, while attempting to "live at peace with everyone" is a step in sanctification that will call for numerous tools in the Christian life, theology nevertheless is a significant aid in this worthwhile endeavor. Before we turn to examine how theology might help us live in peace, let's first give a moment to examine how vital the notion of "peace" is in the Scriptures.

The Scriptural Emphasis on Peace

The Lord is a God of peace. Paul ascribes this title to God in 2 Thessalonians 3:16, "May the *Lord of peace* himself give you peace always in every way." Or, as he says elsewhere, "May the *God of peace* be with all of you" (Rom. 15:33, emphasis added).

Peace with God

Perhaps nothing demonstrates the Lord's commitment to peace more than his covenantal actions among his people. The unfolding drama of the Bible is a story in which God's people—whether the Israelites in the Old Testament or the church in the New Testament—consistently disobey God's commands and wander away from the covenant he made with them. Since God warned that disobeying his law would lead to destruction, he would have been completely justified in giving up on the Israelites early on and letting them receive the destruction they rightfully deserved. Yet this is not how the story unfolds. Instead of getting the punishment they rightfully deserve, God takes it upon himself to bring about peace for his people.

The gospel is nothing short of the news that while we deserved destruction *from* God, through the life, death, and resurrection of Jesus, we instead get peace *with* God. Moreover, peace with God did not come about by a mere sweeping of our disobedience under the rug. On the contrary, as we saw in chapter 2, God pursues peace with his people to the point of death, even death on a cross.

In his letter to the Romans, Paul tells us that "since we have been justified by faith, we have peace with God through our Lord Jesus Christ" (Rom. 5:1). In the person and work of Jesus Christ, we can have the impossible—*peace with God.* The triune God who tells the stars where to hang and the ocean where to stop, who could have left us dead in our trespasses and sins—the gospel tells us we have peace with *him.*

Peace with One Another

In his gospel Jesus not only makes peace between us and God but also makes peace between us and our fellow man. In his letter to the Ephesians, Paul writes of two groups—the Jews and the Gentiles. Historically, these groups had deep-seated animosity with one another, but what we find in the gospel is that "the dividing wall of hostility" between them has been torn down. Through Jesus, they have peace.

Paul writes, "For he is our peace, who made both groups one and tore down the diving wall of hostility. In his flesh, he made of no effect the law consisting of commands and expressed in regulations, so that he might create in himself one new man from the two, *resulting in peace*" (Eph. 2:14–15, emphasis added). Jesus himself is the peace between these two parties. He didn't secure some other thing that reconciles them with one another; he himself is the reconciling agent. How? Because through Christ's death and resurrection, we are, through faith, *united to him.* And if we are united to him by faith, we are united to all others who are united to him.

Our peace with one another is a product of the gospel of peace. As Paul continues to say just a few verses later,

"He came and proclaimed the good news of *peace* to you who were far away and *peace* to those who were near. For through him we both have access in one Spirit to the Father" (Eph. 2:17–18, emphasis added).

In his redemption of an unworthy people, the triune God shows his commitment to peace by making it in two directions: vertically, in bringing sinners into peace with himself, and horizontally, in rewriting the relational realities of his people, so that they might live in harmony with one another.

The scriptural testimony of God being a God of peace and prescribing peace among his people is not confined to the life-changing peace found in the gospel. In fact, the Scriptures have *much* to say about peace. There are far too many references and commands to pursue peace, but even a sampling of what else the Scriptures say about peace will show just how much peace matters to our God.

Almost every letter in the New Testament begins with the author's invoking peace among those who make up the believers in that city. For example, the letters of Romans (1:7), 1 Corinthians (1:3), 2 Corinthians (1:2), Galatians (1:3), Ephesians (1:2), Philippians (1:2), Colossians (1:2), 1 Thessalonians (1:1), 2 Thessalonians (1:2), 1 Timothy (1:2), 2 Timothy (1:2), Titus (1:4), Philemon (1:3), 1 Peter (1:2), 2 John (1:3), 3 John (1:15), Jude (1:2), and Revelation (1:4) all call for peace.[1]

But it is not just in the greetings of the letters where peace shows up. On the contrary, we see the significant emphasis on peace throughout:

- "Peace I leave with you. My peace I give to you. I do not give to you as the world gives. Don't let your heart be troubled or fearful" (John 14:27).
- "I have told you these things so that in me you may have peace. You will have suffering in this world. Be courageous! I have conquered the world" (John 16:33).
- "Let the peace of Christ, to which you were also called in one body, rule your hearts" (Col. 3:15).
- "Finally, brothers and sisters, rejoice. Become mature, be encouraged, be of the same mind, be at peace, and the God of love and peace will be with you" (2 Cor. 13:11).
- "Blessed are the peacemakers, for they will be called sons of God" (Matt. 5:9).

The Old Testament has much to say about peace as well. Again, listing all the Old Testament emphasis on peace would be far too long, but the following are but a few examples:

- "I will both lie down and sleep in peace, for you alone, Lord, make me live in safety" (Ps. 4:8).
- "Abundant peace belongs to those who love your instruction; nothing makes them stumble" (Ps. 119:165).
- "When a person's ways please the Lord, he makes even his enemies to be at peace with him" (Prov. 16:7).
- "May the LORD bless you and protect you; may the LORD make his face shine on you and be gracious to you; may the LORD look with favor on you and give you peace" (Num. 6:24–26).

It should come as no surprise that God's self-revelation in the Scriptures would be riddled with passages calling us to peace since he is indeed the revelation of *the God of peace*. The Bible's significant emphasis on peace shows up in two ways: (1) in particular passages, commands, and encouragements from the Old and New Testament, and (2) in the whole of the biblical drama as God, from Genesis to Revelation, brings about the gospel of grace and creates peace between God and his people and among one another.

Peace in the Mind, Peace in the Soul

Not only does the Bible speak frequently about the importance of peace, but the Scriptures also directly tie the life of the mind to the life of peace. Given that our aim in this chapter is to demonstrate how the contemplation of the Lord in theology leads to peace, we cannot afford to miss three passages. In fact, in looking at these three brief passages, we arrive at the application point of this chapter. Namely, that if theology is done well, it should lead to a life of peace in three significant ways: (1) theology helps us trust God; (2) theology calls us to the kingdom work of peace; and (3) theology aids in establishing *true* unity in the church.

The three passages which explicitly tie together the life of the mind and the life of peace come from the books of Isaiah, Romans, and Philippians. We will recall each of these three passages as we briefly work through the connection between the life of the mind and the life of peace:

1. "You will keep the mind that is dependent on you in perfect peace, for it is trusting in you" (Isa. 26:3).
2. "Now the mindset of the flesh is death, but the mindset of the Spirit is life and peace" (Rom. 8:6).
3. "And the peace of God, which surpasses all understanding, will guard your hearts and minds in Christ Jesus" (Phil. 4:7).

Trusting God

Don't miss the logic of Isaiah 26:3: God keeps whom in perfect peace? *Those whose mind is in perfect peace*. Why? *Because they trust God.*

There is a direct connection between contemplating God and trusting God. Maybe you have experienced a situation where the more you learned about a friend, mentor, or someone you appreciate, the more your respect and admiration for them dwindled. It can be heartbreaking to become acquainted with the shortcomings of your role models.

However, this is never the case with the Lord. On the contrary, it is exactly the opposite. The more we set our mind to the theological task of studying God and all things in relation to God, the more his trustworthiness comes into focus. When God is put under the microscope and his ways analyzed, what comes into focus are not shortcomings but multiplied reasons to trust him.

In book after book in the Scriptures, the Lord demonstrates his steadfast love and trustworthiness. When God's people were enslaved in Egypt, he proved trustworthy; when God's people were wandering in the wilderness, he proved trustworthy; when God's people were taken captive by Assyria and then Babylon and then Persia, he proved trustworthy; when God's people lived through four centuries of silence, he proved trustworthy; when God's people longed eagerly for a Messiah, he proved trustworthy; when God's people needed a once-and-for-all atonement for their sins and shame, he proved trustworthy; when God's people mourned the death of Jesus and his body was sealed in the tomb, he proved trustworthy; as God's people have longed for the return of their King generation after generation, he has proven trustworthy; while God's people await the correction of injustice in the world and long for all wrongs to be made right, he will be proven trustworthy; and on that great day when we see Jesus face-to-face, he will prove trustworthy.

When we set our minds on the things of the Lord and contemplate his being and his ways, peace takes hold of our soul and makes a home. While the world spins into chaos and turmoil, we can be still because our minds are stayed on him. As our minds move toward him, our souls rest in him. In this we find Augustine to be exactly right in his declaration, "Our hearts are restless until they can find rest in you."[2]

The Kingdom Work of Peace

When we take Isaiah up on his advice to set our minds on the Lord and allow peace to take root in our soul, we do not remain the same. As the God of peace opens our eyes to the gospel of peace and our soul rests in the peace of trust, we are compelled to take action. Romans tells us that the mind set on the flesh is death, but a mind set on the Spirit is life and peace (Rom. 8:6).

We would be mistaken, however, to assume that the life and peace that come with setting our mind on the Spirit is a life of inaction, as 2 Corinthians tells us:

> Therefore, if anyone is in Christ, he is a new creation; the old has passed away, and see, the new has come! Everything is from God, who has reconciled us to himself through Christ and has given us the ministry of reconciliation. That is, in Christ, God was reconciling the world to himself, not counting their trespasses against them, and he has committed the message of reconciliation to us.
>
> Therefore, we are ambassadors for Christ, since God is making his appeal through us. We plead on Christ's behalf, "Be reconciled to God." He made the one who did not know sin to be sin for us, so that in him we might become the righteousness of God. (2 Cor. 5:17–21)

When our soul is at peace, we are compelled to join the kingdom work of making peace. The Scripture calls this "the ministry of reconciliation" in which those who have peace with God and one another *plead* with those around them to also find peace with God and one another through the person and work of Jesus Christ.

It is, after all, the "peacemakers" who "will be called sons of God" (Matt. 5:9). As we pursue our calling to be ministers of reconciliation and seek to be peacemakers in the world, it will demand of us to have anchored souls. A mind in a constant state of outrage will lack the needed stability to pursue peace. In our contemplation of God, therefore, may we seek a thoughtful life that we may be numbered among those "peacemakers" who are the true sons and daughters of God.

"Peace, Peace" When There Is No Peace

Theology has another important role to play when establishing peace among God's people—making sure the peace is true.

My personality is bent toward peace. I dislike division and work hard to build bridges instead of burning them. I'm not opposed to difficult discussion or even confrontation, but I'd be lying if I said I enjoyed it. It is much more comfortable for me to appease those around me.

This can even be true of me intellectually. I often find myself looking for a "middle way" in theological arguments or philosophical disagreements. And while *most* of the time, I really do think there is truth somewhere in the middle between the loudest voices, I have been worried that it is by mere personality rather than conviction that I end up in the middle.

I remember recently reading through the book of Jeremiah and being stung by what might have been a passing comment for other readers. In Jeremiah, as Jerusalem refuses to repent of their disobedience against their covenantal God, the Lord's prophet, Jeremiah, rebukes them. In his rebuke, Jeremiah notes that there are those who claim that there is "peace" in the land when there is really no peace at all. The text says, "They have treated my people's brokenness superficially, claiming, *'Peace, peace,' when there is no peace*" (Jer. 6:14, emphasis added).

Theology can aid our endeavors toward peace as it makes sure our peace is not merely a professed peace where there is no real peace to be found. This is why the church, throughout her long history, has sought to develop creeds and confessions. For example, after dealing with false teachers in the third century who claimed that Jesus is not divine like the Father but is a mere creation of the Father, the theologians of the third century came together at Nicaea and formed what we know today as the Nicene Creed. In the Nicene Creed, we read that Jesus is the "only begotten Son of God, begotten from the Father before all time, Light from Light, true God from true God, begotten not created, of the same essence as the Father, through Whom all things came into being."[3]

This theologically rich description of Jesus Christ allowed the churches of the third century to rally around a common teaching about this man from Nazareth. While the council and creed of Nicaea did not end all division, it did give a sturdy foundation for unity and peace in the church. In fact, as I write this, my own local church repeated the Nicene Creed together during our most recent service, showing that even today, some seventeen hundred years later, the theology outlined in this third-century document is still a strong basis for unity.

Nicaea is but one example of how theology can make sure our unity and peace as Christians will not falter like the fake peace of Jeremiah 6. Theology is vital in our drawing the boundary lines for what Christianity *is* and what Christians are *to do*. However, even as we do theology and live our Christian lives within the theological bounds we call orthodoxy, we seek to have the peace of God rule our hearts with all people—regardless of creed or confession (Col. 3:15).

If theology is the study of God and all things in relation to God, and God is the *God of peace* (Rom. 15:33), it would be a deep shame for theologians to go about the business of theologizing in a way that leads not to peace but to division. So then, using theology, we aim to experience the peace Christ has established within our own hearts and then see to it that our theology works itself out, leading to peace among our neighbors.

Chapter Five

Patience

I did not grow up in a Christian home. The gospel and theology were not normal topics of conversation between my family members. Consequently, much of my theological understanding came by conviction, not tradition. I did not inherit a theological system from my parents or grandparents; I had to find one. While I'm thankful that my personal journey from theological ignorance to theological curiosity typically allows me to relate to wherever one is on the theological journey, my story did not come without its hiccups.

One such hiccup came my freshman year of college. I mentioned this episode briefly in chapter 3, but it is a helpful account to relay in more depth here. During my freshman year, I had recently become a Christian and even more recently started contemplating God in a meaningful way. My freshman year was the first time I discovered a love of reading and thinking, which was how I spent much of my time. In that process I experienced something for the first time in my young Christian life—a theological crisis. It was August, and I read something that hit me like a ton of bricks. A theological book said something about God that I had never thought of, and to be honest, I did not much like. This innocent evening of reading sent me into what became a six-month intellectual crisis.

The particularities of what concerned me my freshman year are not important for our discussion here. What is pertinent is that this theological crisis took over my life. It was the first time I had contemplated something about God that kept me awake at night, distracted me from schoolwork, and simply would not leave me be. In those six months, I devoured books, sought council from the elders of my church, listened to podcast episodes and sermons on the topic, attended lectures and debates, and took in just about anything I could get my mind around.

In my crisis of mind, I eventually became a touch exasperated. I so badly wanted to know the truth, and it always seemed just out of reach. Throughout this time, I began to beg the Lord to reveal to me what was true and what was false. As time progressed, my prayers for truth became more desperate. These prayers went from general requests for understanding to pleading with the Lord, "God, I *need* you to reveal yourself here." The longer the confusion and theological fog remained, the more I relied on the Lord to reveal himself to me.

Eventually, the intellectual conundrum I was trapped in relented, and I landed on a position that I thought made sense of the Scripture, the teachings of the church, and my life experience. While coming to a conclusion in the confusion I was feeling was important, what might be even more important than the particularities of my conclusion was what the process taught me. The process of finding myself drowning in doubt and confusion taught me the important lesson of the relationship between theology and patience.

Theological wisdom is not microwavable. To arrive at a place of wisdom in the theological life, you will need wrestling, contemplation, prayer, and patience. This can feel frustrating at times. Maybe you haven't experienced a months-long battle with a question, but you have likely experienced wrestling with a portion of Scripture. Many of us have had the experience of plodding through a passage and feeling inside a notion of "Goodness, I just don't understand this. What am I missing?" Those moments can be filled with frustration, but we should not miss the glory taking place. Often in those moments of longing for understanding, the Lord is at work in us.

In fact, eight words in the book of Hebrews became important to me through that theological crisis my freshman year, and they have been dear to me to this day. In Hebrews 6, the author is telling his or her (scholars are not sure who wrote the book of Hebrews) readers that they need to "leave the elementary doctrine of Christ" and move on to maturity. The author wants these readers to move on from the foundational teaching of Christianity to more sophisticated realities regarding the Christian faith. The author writes,

> Therefore, let us leave the elementary teaching about Christ and go on to maturity, not laying again a foundation of repentance from dead works, faith in God, teaching about ritual washings, laying on of hands, the resurrection of the dead, and eternal judgment. *And we will do this if God permits.* (Heb. 6:1–3, emphasis added)

It is easy to miss that last clause—*this we will do if God permits*—but it holds value we cannot afford to miss. Theological maturity, moving into deeper truths of the Christian faith, is not a right to which we are entitled. Rather, maturing in theological wisdom is all of grace. It is grace that God chooses to reveal himself to us, and it is grace that he allows our minds to be enlightened by his revelation. We will progress into maturity of the mind *if God permits*.

Because of this passage, I teach all my students that the first step in Christian theology is prayer. In theology, it is God we are after, and so it is to God we turn. Not only do we pray at the beginning of trying to understand the Lord but throughout our theological endeavors. Our theological method ought to make much room for prayer, for we will only move on to Christian wisdom if God permits.

"The Limp of Jacob and the Awe of Moses"

Though it can be frustrating and tiresome for us, it seems there are times when the Lord is indeed pleased to permit us knowledge, but only on his time. We might strive for understanding, reading books, discussing with friends, praying and pleading with the Lord, but even in these good endeavors we learn that sometimes what is best is to "be silent before the LORD and wait expectantly for him" (Ps. 37:7).

One theologian, Matthew Levering, described the process of growing in Christian knowledge well when he said that contemplating God requires "the limp of Jacob and the awe of Moses."[1] Jacob and Moses teach us the way of patient and wise theology.

If you're familiar with Jacob's story in the Old Testament, you know that he is involved in a marvelous scene in Genesis 32. In this captivating story, Jacob wrestles with an angel of the Lord. Jacob refuses to let the "man" go until he blesses him, so they wrestle until daybreak. Eventually, the man strikes Jacob's hip, dislocating it and causing him to limp away from the scene. Jacob leaves the incredible scene with a new name—he is now called Israel—and a new limp. Jacob names the sacred place "Peniel" for he has "seen God face to face" and has wrestled with God through the night.

This is a great illustration of how it can feel to progress into Christian wisdom—like a wrestling match. When we come across a tough portion of Scripture, sometimes we must resolve to grab hold of it and, like Jacob, decide we *will not* let go until we see what God has for us to see. Sometimes the process of theology can be described with sophistication and a thoughtful process, but many times the process of Christian theology is simply looking at Christ until you see him.

So we wrestle. We wrestle with words of Scripture; we wrestle with the doctrines of the church; we wrestle in our contemplation and reasoning. At the end of our wrestling, our hope is that we leave with wisdom deep in our soul and with a dislocated hip. These are the marks of someone who has dealt with the Lord.

However, Levering's quote does not end with the limp of Jacob but the awe of Moses. In Exodus 33, Moses is speaking with the Lord outside the camp of God's people on Mount Sinai. In this scene Moses makes a bold request of the Lord: "Please, let me see your glory" (Exod. 33:18). God answers Moses that if he was to see the fullness of God's glory in his face, Moses would surely die. So, instead of allowing Moses to see his face, God hides Moses in the cleft of a rock and passes by him, allowing Moses to catch a glimpse of his back.

Once Moses descends the mountain and returns to the people after speaking with the Lord, the Scriptures say that "the skin of his face shone as a result of his speaking with the LORD" (Exod. 34:29). The sight of Moses's glowing face was so marvelous that it scared the other Israelites, and

Moses had to put a veil over his own face. While the limp of Jacob describes the process of wrestling with God in the task of Christian theology, the awe of Moses describes the aim of Christian theology. In all of our patient wrestling, as we plead with the Lord to reveal his glory to us, we hope to be so transformed that our faces radiate the goodness of our God.

Remember our definition of theology—the study of God and all things in relation to God. This definition has proved important throughout the book already and does so again here. Far from the caricature that theology is something done by academics in ivory towers and has no meaning for our lives, theology is the act of wrestling with God until we see his glory and it transforms our souls.

This wrestling is a lifelong process. Theological wisdom does not happen overnight, and in this way theology is one of the greatest teachers of patience. We must be willing to wrestle with the Scriptures, with theological ideas. And more importantly, we must be willing to let Scripture and theology *wrestle us*. In this back-and-forth, where we wrestle in prayer and in contemplation, the Lord will form us into thinkers spent for his glory and others' good. Yet there is no fast-tracking the process. We ought not attempt to bypass the slow prod toward Christian intellectual maturity; patience is key. With longing and action, we wait on the Lord and call on him to bring about in us a person only he could produce.

Out of Line with Culture, in Line with Scriptures

All nine virtues that make up the fruit of the Spirit are countercultural in some way. This is perhaps especially true of patience.

In fact, it is difficult to choose which cultural artifact is best to use when demonstrating our culture's lack of patience. We are a people who spend hours on multiple screens that demand our ever-shifting attention, a people of same-day deliveries, a people who are largely bored with the pleasures of a good book, a people of microwaved Wikipedia information, and a people simply short on patience. We get antsy when our browsers take more than a few seconds to load or the red light dare last longer than our short attention spans allow. Our social feeds are filled with advertisements that promise to save us time and make every task quicker than it was yesterday.

While our culture "progresses" to eliminate any need for patience, the Scriptures move in the opposite direction. It is no accident that patience appears in the fruit of the Spirit—it is a Christian virtue and one that shows up throughout the biblical drama. God seems to be in no hurry to bring about the full salvation of his people, and as we play a part in God's story of displaying the preeminence of Christ in all things, we must have patience.

Consider the major eras in the story line of Scripture. The people of Israel, as they weave in and out of covenant obedience and suffer the consequences of foreign armies laying siege to their land, longed for a Messiah. The Israelites knew that one day the serpent-crusher would come and set all wrongs to right. Grandfathers told their grandchildren the news of the coming Messiah, and both would perish, along with generations after them, before the Messiah finally showed up in Jesus Christ.

But even before the arrival of Jesus, consider the plight of the people of Israel as the Old Testament comes to a conclusion. Roughly *four hundred years* go by between the time the last prophet stopped speaking and the arrival of Jesus on the scene. God's people had to endure a four-century silence with patience!

However, to see the role and need of patience in God's narrative, you do not even need to look backwards in the story. For we Christians, at this very moment, wait with eagerness for the return of our King, Jesus. While we celebrate the Advent season in the church calendar toward the end of the year, our souls wait in an ongoing season of advent as we proclaim along with John in the book of Revelation, "Come, Lord Jesus!" (Rev. 22:20).

We know that God is all knowing, all good, and all wise, and therefore we know that his prolonging the culmination of history is not an accident. Far be it from the perfect God to make mistakes. On the contrary, God is up to something in the prolonged unfolding of salvation in Jesus Christ. In fact, God is up to a million "somethings." One of them is the production of patience in his people as they long with endurance for the final coming of their king.

Given the significant role the virtue of patience plays throughout the entire drama of Scripture, it is no surprise to see the biblical data riddled with commands to be patient and long-suffering. While it would be beneficial for our souls to do an in-depth study of every occurrence, listing a few instances will have to suffice:

- "Rejoice in hope; be patient in affliction; be persistent in prayer" (Rom. 12:12).
- "Now if we hope for what we do not see, we eagerly wait for it with patience" (Rom. 8:25).
- "With all humility and gentleness, with patience, bearing with one another in love" (Eph. 4:2).
- "But those who trust in the LORD will renew their strength; they will soar on wings like eagles; they will run and not become weary; they will walk and not faint" (Isa. 40:31).
- "Therefore, as God's chosen ones, holy and dearly loved, put on compassion, kindness, humility, gentleness, and patience" (Col. 3:12).
- "The end of a matter is better than its beginning, a patient spirit is better than a proud spirit" (Eccles. 7:8).

- "Therefore, brothers and sisters, be patient until the Lord's coming. See how the farmer waits for the precious fruit of the earth and is patient with it until it receives the early and the late rains. You also must be patient. Strengthen your hearts, because the Lord's coming is near" (James 5:7–8).
- "So that you may not be sluggish, but imitators of those who through faith and patience inherit the promises" (Heb. 6:12 ESV).

From this list of passages and from the endurance the Lord calls his people to throughout the biblical story, we get a small glimpse at just how important this virtue is in the Christian life. While demonstrating patience might put you out of line with our cultural moment, it will nevertheless put you directly in line with biblical faithfulness.

God's Patience Creates Patience

God has been infinitely patient with us. So much so that Peter says, "Regard the patience of our Lord as salvation" (2 Pet. 3:15). While we play around with idols and disregard faithfulness, the Lord is patient and long-suffering in his grace and mercy.

As those who have been immeasurably blessed by the patience of the Lord, we ought to become patient. As we behold the patience of God toward ourselves, we become patient toward our neighbors, our circumstances, and our own spiritual growth.

May we stand out from our instant-gratification culture and be a people eager for patience. Moreover, may theology aid this endeavor. Might the slow plod of learning and contemplating our triune God plant the seeds of patience in our souls.

Chapter Six

Kindness

There is something tremendously tender and sweet about holding your child after praying for years the Lord would give you one. After years of not knowing whether the Lord would grant my and my wife's deep desire to have children, my daughter arrived. Her appearance in the world was a sign of the deep grace of God and a reminder that he is the father of lights who gives good gifts to his children (James 1:17).

During the first year of my daughter's life, one of my favorite ways to pass time was simply to rock her, holding her close and praying over her. Those days I found myself praying two things over her every day. First, I prayed that she would treasure Jesus and cherish his gospel over all things and find in him the greatest adventure and love of her life. Second, I prayed that the Lord would allow her the grace to be wise and kind.

These two adjectives—*wise* and *kind*—came to me the day she was born, and I could not get them out of my head. I knew that if I could pick any two words to describe her, these were the two. But why? Out of all I could have chosen for my firstborn, why were *these* the two words I prayed over her countless times?

There are dozens of reasons I had a desire for my daughter to grow into a wise and kind woman, but one of the many was because I believe wisdom and kindness are two of the most countercultural characteristics in our day.

Our day is an age ruled by much information but little wisdom. We've never been able to access *facts* as quickly as we can right now, and yet I've never felt that we were further from the *truth*. We are short on wisdom, and the voice of lady folly seems ever enticing (Prov. 1–2).

Along with wisdom, ours is a day short on kindness. In the name of the "culture wars," we have relieved ourselves of the call to kindness. Consequently, the casualty of the never-ceasing "culture war" is rarely false ideas but often love for our brothers and sisters. Our news feeds overflow with cutting words composed to gain an audience at the expense of our neighbor. We read those we disagree with in the worst of lights, assume that "our tribe" has the corner on truth, and believe we have little to learn from those with different experiences from our own. We're told that "living our truth" is the most important venture we could set out on and that often the price of getting where we want in life is the devouring of one another.

Into the cultural stream of self-actualization and self-importance, I'm praying my daughter develops a kindness that counts others as more significant than herself (Phil. 2:3). In fact, reader, the prayer I've prayed for my daughter, I've prayed for you. Though nameless to me, as I've constructed this chapter, I've prayed a number of times that the Lord would shape *us all* into the kind of people marked with an unexplainable gospel kindness.

However, if our kindness is based in only a desire to be countercultural, or if our kindness is a strategy *merely to be nice,* I am afraid it will be too fickle and frail to last. In our day we need something deeper than being *merely* nice. Instead, we need an informed kindness—a kindness that is rooted in something larger than our personalities or on whether others *deserve* our kindness. We need a kindness that is an overflow of a transformed heart and an informed mind—a kindness that has taken root deep in our souls, which flavors all our interactions and thoughts of our fellow image bearers. What we need is a theologically informed kindness.

Theologically Informed Kindness

To achieve this vision of a deep kindness, the fruit must be rooted and informed. This is where theology can aid our endeavor of becoming a kind people. The truth of Christian doctrine acts as a rich soil in which we can root our kindness. As we contemplate God and remind ourselves of truth, our mind and soul are reinforced with the realities that nurture a robust kindness. While we could turn to a number of theological realities that might manifest the fruit of kindness in our lives, we here turn our attention to three theological truths—the kindness of God, the wickedness of ourselves, and the *imago Dei* of our brothers and sisters. Setting our mind's eye on these three realities will lead to a "convictional kindness," a theologically informed kindness that will be deeper than mere "niceness" and sturdier than a kindness based on the perceived goodness of others.

The Kindness of the Lord

As we have seen with previous aspects of the fruit of the Spirit, the Lord is the preeminent model of kindness. A close look at God's kindness in the Scriptures shows that sinners like us only have a hope of salvation because our God is kind. Douglas Moo, commenting on Paul's use of the word *kindness*, points out that the apostle often uses this word "to denote God's gracious response to his rebellious creation (Rom. 2:4, 11:22; Eph. 2:7; Titus 3:4; cf. Pss. 31:19, 68:10, 119:68)."[1]

God's kindness is a lightning bolt that strikes our dead hearts and calls us to life. This is why Paul can say, in Romans 2:4, that we ought not presume on God's kindness, for "God's kindness is intended to lead you to repentance." We often think what finally breaks our rebellion against God is his wrath against us. This is reflected in the way we treat others who frustrate us. If we yell at them or give them the cold shoulder, eventually they'll figure it out and do the right thing. But how's that working for us?

On the contrary, in the face of God's *kindness* we bend the knee and turn toward him. What makes God's loving-kindness in the Scriptures so remarkable is that he lavishes even his enemies with kindness. While we fail to show kindness to those closest and dearest to us, God is kind to those who despise him.

Ephesians 2 is a perfect picture of God's remarkable kindness toward the undeserving. It opens by describing our helpless estate before God, *"You were dead in your trespasses and sins"* (v. 1). In our "deadness" we walked according to the world and followed the "ruler of the power of the air" (v. 2) and in so doing have become "children under wrath" (v. 3). Yet the good news of the Christian gospel is that God did not leave us in our helpless estate, but he came after us. Ephesians 2:4–5 picks up, "But God, who is rich in mercy, because of his great love that he had for us, made us alive with Christ even though we were dead in trespasses. You are saved by grace!"

As if being delivered from death to life was not good news enough, Ephesians continues with a stunning truth: God lavishes his children with kindness. Verse 7 says God has raised us up with Christ "so that in the coming ages he might display the immeasurable riches of his grace through his kindness to us in Christ Jesus." Don't miss the transformation in Ephesians 2. In just seven verses all who are united to Christ move from those who are "dead in trespasses and sins" to those who are seated with Christ in resurrected glory—all that God might show his immeasurable riches of grace and kindness.

Our God is profoundly kind, and we are the undeserving beneficiaries. In the cosmic kindness of our God, we find an eternal example of what a life of kindness looks like.

The Wickedness in Ourselves

The Scriptures often act like a mirror. When we look to them to see our true selves, it can be a bit disheartening.

We learn that apart from Christ, as we have seen above, we are "dead in [our] trespasses and sins" (Eph. 2:1). Moreover, we see that "the heart is more deceitful that anything else" (Jer. 17:9). In our natural state we set our minds on the flesh and therefore desire the things of the flesh. In this helpless estate, we could never understand the things of the light, nor could we ever please God (Rom. 8:5; 1 Cor. 2:14).

In short, in our natural state we are all wicked. No one is free from this pronouncement, as Paul makes clear: "There is no one righteous, not even one. There is no one who understands; there is no one who seeks God" (Rom. 3:10–11). Given that we all share the same condition—that none of us seek God on our own—we also all share in the same consequence, "For all have sinned and fall short of the glory of God. . . . For the wages of sin is death" (Rom. 3:23; 6:23).

In Christian theology, we call this doctrine *total depravity.* By this term we do not mean that all people are as bad as they could possibly be. Rather, what we mean by the term *total depravity* is that we are *thoroughly* depraved. There is not a portion of our being that is untainted from the brutal effects of sin, not a portion of our being that doesn't need the redemption offered in Christ. So, then, what do the doctrine of total depravity and our own wickedness have to do with kindness?

Having a theological foundation for the wickedness that resides in us and in those around us helps us establish a kind heart in a few ways. First, when we experience unkindness from strangers or those close to us, we can resolve not to retaliate. The sad reality about us all being impacted by sin is that even those we love to have the capacity to act in ways brutally inconsistent with righteousness—often with the consequence of inflicting pain on those around them. The Scriptures have given us a blueprint of the human soul, and when the soul acts in accordance with the flesh, we ought not be overly surprised and crave retaliation.

This leads to the second point: just as sin resides in those we love, which gives them the capacity to act unkindly toward us, we know that the same sin resides in us. This awareness should give us pause so that we can pray for mercy and help from God to act so that we respond to unkind acts with kindness rather than retaliating or seeking vengeance.

Those whose kindness is rooted in rich theological soil, instead of personal preferences or personalities, can withstand a storm of unkindness and respond with kindness. For we are aware enough of sin's impact on us to know we are just a couple of bad decisions away from displaying the same unkindness.

The Imago Dei *in Others*

Another doctrine might help anchor kindness deep in our soul—the *imago Dei*. If the *wickedness in us* helps us be kind by being an understanding and forgiving people, the *imago Dei* in others helps us value them as those who bear God's image. Both doctrines add important ingredients to a theologically informed kindness. The doctrine of total depravity develops empathy and care for others while the doctrine of the *imago Dei* develops value and appreciation for others.

What is the doctrine of the *imago Dei*? The phrase *imago Dei* is a Latin phrase that means "the image of God." When God created the world, he marked the pinnacle of creation—man and woman—with his image. Genesis 1 tells us, "So God created man in his own image, he created him in the image of God; he created them male and female" (Gen. 1:27). Furthermore, we read later in Genesis that "whoever sheds human blood, by humans his blood will be shed, *for God made humans in his image*" (Gen. 9:6, emphasis added).

Everyone you know, from the closest relative to the farthest stranger, is marked and made in the image of God. This means that everyone you know has deep and meaningful value. While the wickedness that resides in the shadows of our soul might make it tempting to treat others as less than yourself, the image of God means that no matter who we are dealing with, kindness is the way forward.

Bringing the image of God into the conversation of theologically informed kindness is important because rooting kindness in the doctrine of the *imago Dei* means that we do not display kindness only if people have *earned* it by their actions. Rather, we live our lives with the conviction that our kindness should fall on everyone because they *deserve* it, not based on their actions but on their very nature. Because of the one who made them and in whose image they reside, we are to treat all our neighbors with love and kindness.

"Convictional Kindness"

In his 2015 book *Onward,* Russell Moore used a phrase that has stuck with me, one that this chapter seeks to promote. Moore argued that Christians ought to have a "convictional kindness."[2] Summarizing this important phrase, Moore writes, "Convictional kindness means loving people enough to tell them the truth, and to tell ourselves the truth about them."[3]

We are people of conviction because we love the truth. We love that God has said what is right and what is wrong. We love that he has revealed himself in propositions *and* story. We love that the Christian faith comes with truth claims that must be affirmed. We love that this is a faith of *conviction*. However, we not only love truth, but we also love people. We love those who, like us, have wickedness dwelling in the shadows of their soul and who, nevertheless, bear the image of our Creator.

The way forward for a theologically informed kindness is the path that seeks to uphold a deep love for both convictional theology and our image-bearing neighbors. We are not those who shrink back from telling the truth, and we are not those who shrink back from being kind to our fellow man. Rather, in a world of cyclical outrage and a ceaseless devouring of one another, we march forward, with the kindness of God as our example, and strive to be the kind of people who choose a countercultural kindness. This only comes from a radical understanding of the gospel of Jesus Christ.

This vision of Christian wisdom, in which the spiritual fruit of kindness lives deep in our soul, is much stronger than a mere *niceness*. A theologically informed kindness is a *rooted* kindness. It is not passive and weak but active in its understanding of God and all things in relation to God, such that we can make sense of our world and be wise in our interaction with others.

Chapter Seven

Goodness

In his masterpiece of a children's series, The Chronicles of Narnia, C. S. Lewis paints a number of beautiful and illuminating scenes. One such scene comes in the book *The Magician's Nephew*. A few characters find themselves in an empty world of nothingness. However, as they inhabit this void and empty world, something breaks the silence in the distance. The noise causes some of the characters to sit in wonder while others feel disgust.

The sound they hear is the voice of Aslan the great lion, the character in Lewis's series who represents Christ. The magnificent beast is *singing*. As the characters hear the great lion's voice, it becomes apparent to them what is happening—Aslan is singing Narnia into existence. With the beauty of his voice, Aslan creates Narnia, and neither the characters nor the setting of the story will ever be the same.[1]

As magnificent as this scene is in Narnia, and as magnificent as I'm sure the fictional lion's voice was in the ears of the first king and queen of Narnia, it holds no candle to the reality of Genesis 1:1. Fiction is incredible. Yet part of its wonder is that it tries to capture and articulate beauty that it has no jurisdiction over. For, while fiction can be beautiful, God's reality is infinitely more majestic and awe inducing. Fiction is simply the schoolmaster of beauty, which is a shadow of the real beauty behind God's actual world.

In the opening salvo of Christian Scripture, we read: "In the beginning God created the heavens and the earth" (Gen 1:1). This earth had no form and was void. No material already existed. God didn't stumble upon the basic building blocks of the cosmos and simply rearrange them to create our world. Rather, *out of nothing,* God calls forth creation and the order therein. By the word of his power, God brings what was not there into existence.

This powerful and majestic God, by simply speaking, calls forth stars and tells them where to hang. God calls forth the oceans and tells them where to stop. God calls forth both animals of the water and animals of the land and gives them beauty and uniqueness. God calls forth vegetation and the flowers of the earth. He establishes colors and smells. He brings forth mountains and valleys. All we see and could ever see, he speaks it out of nothing. Then, on the final day of creation, he brings forward mankind—man and woman.

As each day of creation passes by, the Scriptures repeat a vital phrase. After each of the first five days of creation, the Scriptures tell us that God looked over what he created and "God saw that it was *good*" (Gen. 1:25, emphasis added). This formula is only broken on the sixth day. When God creates man and woman, the Scriptures add a word of superlative to the formula. On this final day of creation, after looking at the creation of mankind, the Scriptures say, "God saw all that he had made, and it was *very good* indeed" (Gen 1:31, emphasis added).

The doctrine of creation is a test case for goodness. Everything God called forth out of nothing was good, and indeed it was *very good*. The land and water, the fish and the birds, the vegetables and the fruit, the man and the woman—all of it was *good*.

The Good Creator

The goodness of creation should not surprise us because it was brought out of nothing by a good Creator. God's good world is rooted in God's own goodness, which is attested to throughout the Scriptures.[2]

Of God's goodness in the Scriptures, we read that when we dwell in the house of the Lord, goodness and mercy will pursue us all the days of our lives (Ps. 23:6). We see that those who take refuge in the Lord are blessed, as they will "taste and see that the LORD is good" (Ps. 34:8). We read that the Lord is not only good in his very being, but that he also does good. Again, the psalmist puts this important reality into words by saying explicitly, "You are good, and you do what is good; teach me your statutes" (Ps. 119:68).

We also read that every good gift comes down from our "Father of lights, who does not change" (James 1:17). Not only is God good, but he is unchangeably good. He will not increase as to add goodness to himself, and he will not decrease as to take goodness away from himself. Rather, God is perfectly good; he need not and indeed *cannot* increase or decrease in his goodness. Finally, in discussing God's goodness, it is important to remind ourselves of the vital doctrine we covered in chapter 1—divine simplicity. God does not merely *have* goodness as if it were something he could gain or lose. Rather, God *is* good. His very being is the definition of goodness.

This is why, in the strange and glorious passage of Exodus 33, when Moses asks to see the Lord, the Lord replies that Moses cannot see his face or else Moses would die. Instead, God says that he will hide Moses in the cleft of the rock and "cause all *my goodness* to pass in front of you" (Exod. 33:19, emphasis added). God's very being is good, and therefore it makes sense for God to say that "his goodness" is passing by Moses in that glorious scene on Mount Sinai.

In the doctrine of creation and in the doctrine of God, we see that we inhabit a good world created by a good God.

Goodness in the Life of Our Souls

The doctrine of God's own goodness and the goodness of God's created world provides a solid theological foundation to demonstrate how theology should lead to goodness in the life of our soul. As humans, we are hardwired to desire the good. Because we are God's creatures and he is good in his very being, and because we inhabit a world in which goodness is built into the fabric of its existence, our souls long for goodness.

Previously, we discussed "the transcendentals." As a reminder, the transcendentals are those things that transcend our tangible and pragmatic existence and for which all humans long. Namely, we desire the transcendental realities of the good, the true, and the beautiful. These three realities pull us outside of ourselves and remind us that the world is bigger than our day-to-day problems.

Wisdom in our world, at least in part, should be identified by individuals' ability to consistently remind themselves of and find the good, the true, and the beautiful in our world. Many of us get so absorbed in what is immediately in front of us—the anxieties of the day, the pragmatics of possessions, the utilitarian view of life, which only sees value in what can be used—that we lose sight of the transcendentals. We know the instability that comes from these items is not Christian wisdom, yet we often fail to get our eyes past those things and onto the most important things. Don't misunderstand—I'm not saying we should *ignore* or *avoid* what's directly in front of us (as if we could). However, those who go about their life still mindful of the people and places directly in front of them but who nevertheless keep their mind's eye on the good, the true, the beautiful are the ones who have nuance, stability, and a wisdom the world desires.

Christian wisdom gets us at much more than simply how much money I can make, how much fame I can foster, how many possessions I can accumulate, and how much applause I can garner. Christian wisdom pulls our gaze outward and upward, to deeper and more consequential realities—like the transcendentals.

It is helpful to see where this desire of ours comes from. Theology not only helps us place our desire for the good in its proper home—the doctrine of God and the doctrine of creation—but it also helps us foster it. The more we contemplate God's goodness—a goodness that is identical with *who he is*—the more we will want to see the good that is around us.

You may have heard the advice, "Don't be so heavenly minded that you are no earthly good." But what I'm proposing here seeks to flip this advice on its head. What I'm proposing here is that you *should* be heavenly minded and you *should* cast your mind's eye on God's goodness such that you are captivated by his beauty and glory. Then you can't help but do and see goodness in the world around you.

Do Not Grow Weary and Be Zealous

Beyond developing an appetite for the good, the true, and the beautiful, how might a theology of goodness lead to goodness in our soul? The answer comes in the form of obedience to Scripture's many commands to pursue goodness. Not only does the Bible give us a grand vision for a goodness of *being,* but it also gives us a grand vision for a goodness of *doing.*

Three particular passages come to mind: 1 Peter 3:13; Galatians 6:9; and Micah 6:8.

First Peter 3:13 asks a provocative question, "Who then will harm you if you are devoted to what is good?" Galatians 6:9 commands us not to view pursuing good as a temporary command but rather to "not get tired of doing good, for we will reap at the proper time if we don't give up." These two passages come together to command us to be zealous to do good and not to grow weary in our zeal for goodness. Our pursuit of goodness is lifelong. Only when we are gripped by a theology of God's grand goodness can we have a fuel for goodness to prevent us from growing weary.

This fuel that prevents us from growing weary helps us pursue a Micah 6:8 kind of life. Micah 6:8 instructs us: "Mankind, he has told each of you what is good and what it is the LORD requires of you: to act justly, to love faithfulness, and to walk humbly with your God."

When we contemplate God's goodness in our mind, and the beauty therein compels us to pursue goodness with our hands, the beneficiary should be our neighbors. As those who long for goodness and have seen goodness in the Lord, we pursue the good of others by doing justice, loving kindness, and walking humbly with God. We are those who, when confronted with the question of Cain—"Am I my brother's keeper?" (Gen 4:9 ESV)—answer with an emphatic yes! We *are* our brothers' keepers and happily so. As those who have been gripped by the goodness of God, we pour ourselves out for the good of those around us.

How might this theologically informed concern for the good of our neighbors manifest itself in our lives? A few ways.

We pursue our neighbor's good with our speech. As Ephesians 4:29 commands us, "No foul language should come from your mouth, *but only what is good for building up* someone in need, so that it gives grace to those who hear" (emphasis added). A consistent theme in this book has been the importance of our speech, and it is no different here. We can pursue the good of our neighbors with the goodness of our words.

What does your speech reveal about how you view your neighbor? Are you consistently belittling others with your speech? Do you seek to reveal their shortcomings to establish your own supposed superiority? Or does your speech build up your brothers and sisters in the Lord? In your words, could others find life? In your words, could others find the bread crumbs of the bread of life? Slander, belittling, biting sarcasm, unhelpful critique, and hurtful exaggeration should all be far from us as we seek to love our neighbor with our speech. The Lord has given us a powerful tool in the tongue. May we bend our words toward the good of others and the glory of God.

We pursue our neighbor's good with our time and possessions. This one is hopefully obvious. For "the one who has two shirts must share with someone who has none, and the one who has food must do the same" (Luke 3:11). Your possessions and your time are not your own; like all things, they belong to the Lord. Moreover, your time and your possessions can be powerful instruments of good. God has not called you to a life of isolation, apart from your neighbors, and he has not called you to a life of accumulation. On the contrary, he has called you to a life of generosity, and your time and possessions are vital means toward that end.

We pursue our neighbor's good by pursuing justice. In our pursuit of the good, we must be careful that we keep our minds on what is *actually* good. We do not want to become like those mentioned in Isaiah 5 "who call evil good and good evil, who substitute darkness for light and light for darkness, who substitute bitter for sweet and sweet for bitter" (v. 20). Instead of calling "good" that which is evil in the world, we want to seek the good by seeing "justice flow like water, and righteousness, like an unfailing stream" (Amos 5:24).

As Christians, setting our minds on the *good* should lead to a life concerned with justice as we aim for the good of those who have been abused, marginalized, and mistreated.

Consider how Deuteronomy describes our God: "For the LORD your God is the God of gods and Lord of lords, the great, mighty, and awe-inspiring God, showing no partiality and taking no bribe. *He executes justice for the fatherless and the widow, and loves the resident alien, giving him food and clothing.* You are also to love the resident alien, since you were resident aliens in the land of Egypt" (Deut. 10:17–19, emphasis added). Like our God, may we be about the good of the fatherless, the widow, and the sojourner.

We pursue our neighbor's good with the gospel. Even more important than our time and possessions (but not to the exclusion of them), the most important thing we can give our neighbor is the gospel. If it is bad to see your neighbor thirsty and refuse to give him water, it is worse to see your neighbor perishing and refuse to give him the living water!

The Psalms have featured heavily in this chapter, and we return to them once again. In Psalm 25:7 the psalmist pleas, "Do not remember the sins of my youth or my acts of rebellion; in keeping with your faithful love, remember me *because of your goodness,* LORD" (emphasis added). Because of God's goodness, our sins are paid for in the death of Jesus. Once we've experienced that goodness, we cannot help but take it to others. If we care for the good of our neighbors, we will care to see them possess the treasure of treasures—Jesus Christ himself.

Seeing Good and Doing Good

Christopher Holmes writes, "The experience of God's goodness evokes spiritual gladness."[3] May it be so with us. As theology is the study of God and all things in relation to God, when we go about the business of Christian theology, we cannot help but get an eyeful of the good. In our contemplation of God and his goodness, may we become people who *see good and do good.* May the contemplation of the good in our minds lead to seeking the good with our hands. May the fruit of the Spirit that is goodness find a place in our soul as we reflect on the theology of God's good world and God's goodness in himself.

Chapter Eight

Faithfulness

On that great and final day when the Lord comes back to judge the living and the dead, we all hope to hear from the lips of our King, "Well done, good and faithful servant!" (Matt. 25:23). Before we can hear the final pronouncement of faithfulness on that day of judgment, we have scores of days in front of us in which we must prove faithful.

Faithfulness is a fruit of the Spirit that waxes and wanes throughout our lives. Some days we might prove faithful to the Lord and his call on our life, while others we may come up wanting. As we are conformed, from one degree to another (2 Cor. 3:18), into the image of the one who was supremely faithful, we need as many tutors in the school of faithfulness as we can recruit. In our journey of following Christ and in our call to be holy as he is holy (Lev. 19:2; 1 Pet. 1:16), the road to faithfulness calls for endurance. On this adventure, theology can play an important role.

We could examine many aspects in exploring theology's relationship with faithfulness, but I'd like to focus on two primary ones. Namely, Christian theology aids us on our journey toward the spiritual fruit of faithfulness by *reminding* us of the faithfulness of God and *reinforcing* our own faithfulness.

Remembering God's Faithfulness

"What do those stones mean to you?" According to Joshua 4:6, this is the question the people of Israel hoped their children would ask them as they erected a monument to the Lord consisting of twelve stones. The Lord commanded his people in the Old Testament to march toward the promised land, which he was preparing for them. On the journey toward this land, obstacles arose, including the physical obstacle of getting over the Jordan River. After the death of their first leader, Moses, the people of Israel followed Joshua as he led them toward the land God had promised. Yet the people faced the significant issue that they had to find a way to cross this body of water to get there.

When the Israelites got to the bank of the Jordan and came face-to-face with their daunting challenge—the water that prohibited their progress—they saw God come through in a major way. The Scriptures tell us that God allowed them to pass on dry ground as he caused the waters to rise "up in a heap very far away" (Josh. 3:16 ESV). This miraculous move from God allowed all the Israelites to pass over the Jordan on dry ground. After the entire nation passed over without any problem, Joshua was commanded to instruct twelve of his men to grab a stone from the river (representing the twelve tribes of Israel). The men did as instructed. Each hoisted a large stone upon his shoulder. With the stones, the people of Israel built a monument to remind them of God's faithfulness in bringing them safely across the Jordan on the way to the promised land.

When their children grew up one day and asked their parents, "What do these stones mean to you?" The people were instructed: "You should tell them, 'The water of the Jordan was cut off in front of the ark of the LORD's covenant. When it crossed the Jordan, the Jordan's water was cut off." The Scripture concludes by saying of the stones, "These stones will always be a memorial for the Israelites" (Josh. 4:7).

These twelve stones were more than mere rocks. They were a reminder for the people of Israel and generations of their children that God provided for them when all hope seemed lost.

A Forgetful People

To our discredit and often to our detriment, we are a forgetful people. While the twelve stones in the story above primarily serve the purpose of being a teaching lesson for the children of those who crossed the Jordan, we are often in desperate need of reminders in our own lives.

This is why "remember" is such an oft-quoted command in the Scriptures. In fact, the Scriptures are sandwiched with a similar command to remember the Lord and what he has done for his people. Toward the beginning of Scripture, in Deuteronomy 6, Moses instructs God's people, "Be careful not to forget the LORD who brought you out of the land of Egypt, out of the place of slavery" (Duet. 6:12). Toward the end of the Scriptures, in Jude, this command is picked up again, "Now I want to remind you, although you came to know all these things once and for all, that Jesus saved a people out of Egypt and later destroyed those who did not believe" (Jude 5). From the beginning of our story, in Deuteronomy, toward the end of the biblical journey, in Jude's epistle, God's people are a people in constant need of remembering and reminding.

We are the kind of people with the mental capacity to remember an avalanche of anxiety, but we have intellectual amnesia when it comes to recalling God's faithfulness. Our minds are skilled at gravitating toward that which will not aid our pursuit of faithfulness. On the contrary, our minds need training to "remember" that God is good in himself and good in his actions toward us. Your heart will not drift toward faithfulness; it will take discipline to set your mind's eye on God's glory.

Like the Israelites crossing the Jordan River into the promised land, we need reminders of God's faithfulness throughout our journey. It is here that theology can play a significant role.

What Do These Doctrines Mean to You?

Like those twelve stones stacked on the bank of the Jordan River, theology can act as a signpost to remind God's people that he is faithful. Within theology individual teachings of the Christian faith are often called "doctrines." We, as God's people, have an embarrassment of riches when it comes to doctrines that can stir our minds to remember God's faithfulness.

A great example of a Christian doctrine that can act as a "stone" or a signpost to remind us of God's faithfulness is the doctrine of "imputed righteousness." In its most basic form, the doctrine of imputed righteousness deals with the reality that the righteousness needed for salvation Jesus not only obtains for us in his life and death but gives to us in our union with him.

As we saw earlier, we are dead in our trespasses and sins, as we've all fallen short of the glory of God. All of us, like our first parents Adam and Eve, have sunk our treacherous teeth into the forbidden fruit of sinfulness. Like rebels, we have all traded the glorious freedom of righteousness for the slavish bonds of disobedience against God. As we have wandered away from our true home and taken the way of death, we have put enmity between ourselves and God and cultivated hearts of stone. In sum, we put ourselves in a helpless estate of sin and shame.

But God saw our helpless estate, and he *did* something about it.

God saw our determination to run away from him and, like the hound of heaven he is, he came after us. Because God is himself holiness, he could not simply ignore our wickedness and rebellion against him. Nor, again due to his holiness, could he simply allow us back into Eden with our guilt still hanging around our necks. God will not keep company with the unrighteous, and if our ultimate hope is eternal company with our good King, righteousness is what we desperately needed.

In the coming of the second person of the Trinity—Jesus Christ—we see not only "God is with us" but our only hope of righteousness (Isa. 7:14; Matt. 1:23). When Jesus took on flesh (which we will discuss in just a few pages), he lived his life in perfect obedience to the Father and the Father's law. Every second Jesus spent on earth, he spent in perfection. No wrong thought, no wrong deed, no wrong word, and no wrong action ever came from him. The track record of all human history from the first days was disobedience until that man Christ Jesus came in the flesh.

He saw our helpless estate at achieving the righteous requirements of the law, and he obtained them by his own merit. Jesus's fulfilling the righteous requirements of God's law would not be good news to us if he kept the merits to himself. The prize of Jesus's perfect life should have been a continued perfect blessedness and glorification. However, as we traded our graveclothes for his robes of righteousness, he took the penalty for our disobedience, and we took the prize for his righteousness. Because the righteousness of Christ is ours, we are God's children; we can come to him not as unwanted but as those who are adopted and treasured members of the family. Because of Christ's righteousness given to us, we can approach the throne with boldness, knowing that the Father will never turn away his Son, and we are united to that Son.

This is a brief discussion of the doctrine theologians call imputed righteousness, but even in this brief discussion we see how this doctrine acts as a signpost to remind us of God's faithfulness toward us. Like the children of the Israelites in the day of Joshua would ask of their parents, "What do these stones mean to you?" we can examine the beautiful doctrines that comprise Christian theology and ask, *"What do these doctrines mean to you?"*

The aim of this chapter is to show that the answer to this question should not be altogether different from the answer those Israelite fathers and mothers gave their children: we set our minds on Christian doctrines and tend to the work of contemplating the beauty therein because in them we see the million gears of grace God is turning as he wins his bride.

As the stack of twelve stones was to serve as a reminder until the people of Israel reached the promised land, we lay hold of God's truth as a reminder of his faithfulness until we reach our own promised land. Generations will come and generations will go; through each one may we point to our own doctrinal stack of stones and teach our kids of the Lord's faithfulness.

Reinforcing Our Faithfulness

While Christian theology can serve as a powerful reminder of God's faithfulness, its value lies not only in *reminding us of God's faithfulness in the past* but also in *reinforcing our own faithfulness in the present and future.* How might theology reinforce our own faithfulness in following the Lord? Allow me to illustrate by virtue of a personal story. In this story I hope to contrast two different conversations. Both of these conversations were about motivating Christians to join the important work of international missions.

In the first scenario, I was watching a fundraising pitch given by a friend in hopes of gaining support for a six-month trip overseas. The friend was nearing the completion of funding his trip and was giving a presentation to a group of us who were considering funding his group. In the presentation, a dear brother used a PowerPoint slide to demonstrate the poverty that existed where their team was hoping to visit. In slide after slide, we saw heart-wrenching pictures of children with potbellies from a lack of food and were given stats about access to basic humanitarian necessities for this remote village. It was stirring and effective in fundraising efforts. No one in the room left that night's presentation without a burden on his heart. The images and stats were hard to shake, and they took a good portion of my thought life the next few days.

The second scenario comes from the first time I ever read J. I. Packer's masterful work, *Knowing God*. In one portion of the book, Packer describes what he calls "the Christmas spirit," which counts others as more significant than themselves. Packer argues that Christians ought to have this Christmas spirit year-round. He writes:

> The Christmas spirit does not shine out in the Christian snob. For the Christmas spirit is the spirit of those who, like their Master, live their whole lives on the principle of making themselves poor—spending and being spent—to enrich their fellowmen, giving time, trouble, care and concern to do good to others—and not just their own friends—in whatever way there seems need.[1]

When my eyes worked across these words for the first time as a freshman in college, they stung. I felt a deep conviction about what life would look like if our days were marked by "making ourselves poor—spending and being spent—to enrich their fellowmen."

This powerful line called to my mind the second chapter of Philippians. Paul opens the second chapter of his letter to the Philippians by instructing the Christians there, saying, "If, then, there is any encouragement in Christ, if any consolation of love, if any fellowship with the Spirit, if any affection and mercy, make my joy complete by thinking the same way, having the same love, united in spirit, intent on one purpose" (Phi. 2:1–2). Paul continues to instruct the Philippians that they can fulfill this command by following Christ's example, which is worth quoting at length:

> Do nothing out of selfish ambition or conceit, but in humility consider others as more important than yourselves. Everyone should look not to his own interests, but rather to the interests of others. Adopt the same attitude as that of Christ Jesus, who, existing in the form of God, did not consider equality with God as something to be exploited. Instead he emptied himself by assuming the form of a servant, taking on the likeness of humanity. And when he had come as a man, he humbled himself by becoming obedient to the point of death—even to death on a cross. For this reason God highly exalted him and gave him the name that is above every name, so that at the name of Jesus every knee will bow—in heaven and on earth and under the earth—and every tongue will confess that Jesus Christ is Lord, to the glory of God the Father. (Phil. 2:3–11)

Notice how Paul's words here to the Philippians are echoed in Packer's call for us to have the "Christmas spirit." Paul describes Christ as the one who *"emptied himself,"* and though he was *"in the form of God,"* he took *"the form of a servant."* Christ emptied himself and allowed himself to be humbled, even to the point of death—death on a cross.

Christ is the supreme example of Packer's "Christmas spirit." Christ is the ultimate example of one who lived on the principle of spending and being spent for the good of his brothers and sisters. Though Christ has always been found in the form of God (since he is the eternal Son, not made but begotten, as the Nicene Creed states), he humbled himself and took on flesh. We call this the doctrine of the incarnation. Christ, while remaining truly God, became truly man by taking on flesh assuming the form of a servant. Christ was made poor in his flesh that we might be made rich in his righteousness and grace.

While discussing these beautiful truths, another dear friend felt called to international missions. In his mind the doctrine of the incarnation—in which Christ did not revel in his rights but instead saw our helpless estate and stepped into the brokenness of our life—was a model for missionary work. My friend could have stayed in the States; he could have likely taken a great ministry job and lived the ministerial version of the American dream. However, the doctrine of the incarnation haunted him in all the right ways. The divine action in which the second person of the Trinity took on flesh and met us in our need became a model for him to forsake his rights and meet others in their need—wherever in the world that may lead him.

In this way theology reinforced his faithfulness. I do not intend here to make light of the first scenario of those scarring images. I actually think it is right and good for Christians to see injustice in the world and want to do something about it. However, as I have reflected on and contrasted those two stories of international missions, I cannot help but hope the latter example becomes the norm.

You see, the guilt and pain that rise up from horrifying pictures or disturbing statistics will likely be enough to *get* you to the mission field, but guilt and pain will never *keep you on mission*. Only a theologically robust gospel message can do that. It takes something as grand as the news that Jesus Christ the righteous took on flesh that we might be made right with God to reinforce our faithfulness over our lifetimes.

Remind and Reinforce, Again and Again

Missions is, of course, but a single example of how theology reinforces our current faithfulness in following the Lord. In fact, there is enough beauty in the theological life to find the fuel needed to reinforce faithfulness in every facet of the Christian life. A life spent contemplating God and all things in relation to God is a life well spent, for doing so will both recall to our mind's eye the multitude of times the Lord has proven faithful and will reinforce in us our own faithfulness in following him. So, whether your life's calling is the mission field, business, education, parenting, pastoral ministry, medicine, or anything else—the beauty of Christian theology can be a well for you to drink from in order to reinforce your faithfulness for the rest of your days.

It is important to note, however, in the close of this chapter, that there is a direct relationship between the two aspects of faithfulness we have been discussing in this chapter. Theology should indeed reinforce our faithfulness in all areas of our life. However, because we, like the people of Israel, are a forgetful people, we will need to remind ourselves of God's truth, and then remind ourselves of them again, and then remind again and again.

At various times in this book, I've called theology a well of joy. Like any well, theology is a well to be visited time and again. We ought to be a people who think hard and think often, a people who read deep and read wide. For, in re-plumbing the beautiful depths of theological beauty we will be reminded of God's faithfulness to us and, in turn, have our faithfulness toward him reinforced.

Chapter Nine

Gentleness

The world is upside down. We think we perceive our surroundings rightly, but when we have the eyes of the kingdom, we realize much of what seems "normal" is the exact opposite of reality.

A great example of this upside-down world comes in a collection of Puritan prayers called *The Valley of Vision*. This collection is a series of prayers from saints of the past. The first one serves as an important teacher of a world flipped right side up. In the prayer, the Puritans say:

> Let me learn by paradox:
> that the way down is the way up,
> that to be low is to be high,
> that the broken heart is the healed heart,
> that the contrite spirit is the rejoicing spirit,
> that the repenting soul is the victorious
> soul,
> that to have nothing is to possess all,

> that to bear the cross is to wear the crown,
> that to give is to receive,
> that the valley is the place of vision.[1]

Jesus teaches us that the world is upside down right now, but one day, as Christ's kingdom comes, everything will be turned right side up. In *that* kingdom those "who are first will be last, and the last first" (Matt. 19:30). In this world, it seems right to us that the *powerful* are those who are qualified to lead. Out of sheer strength and dogged determination, you get what you want in our world. We have cultivated a "win at all costs" mentality and train ourselves to assert our might toward our desired ends, crushing anything that stands in our way. However, the Scripture paints a contrasting kingdom in which the meek will inherit the earth (Matt. 5:5; Ps. 37:11).

The Upside-Down Kingdom

It is a marvel when the gospel brings about the change of sight by virtue of our new birth. When the veil that covers our perception of how the world actually works is torn in two by the work of Jesus and we see that the way of increase is through the path of decrease, the gospel has transformed our blindness into sight. The gospel gives us a kingdom perspective in which we see the glorious reversal of an upside-down world.

Theology can here provide a glorious interruption to what we see every day before us. Christian theology is something of an optometrist, diagnosing our nearsightedness and prescribing the lenses of the kingdom of God. A robust understanding of the kingdom, and its King, helps bring *reality* into focus. While what is in front of us seems and feels real, it is not.

It is not true, for example, that self-actualization is the most important venture for you to set out on. It is not true that weakness is a vice to be avoided. As we contemplate life as a citizen of God's kingdom, theology helps the mirage of lies fall, and in its place stands the true, the good, and the beautiful.

As we grow into our kingdom eyes and see the world as it actually is, where the last are first, one reality that comes into focus is that gentleness is not weakness but strength. The ethics of Christ's kingdom teach us that the path to greatness is not through power but through gentleness and meekness. Again, it is not the powerful who will inherit the earth but the *meek*. The ethics and theology of God's kingdom take our upside-down world and set it back in right order.

The King of This Kingdom

In learning the theology of the kingdom of God, it helps to turn our gaze toward the kingdom's King—Jesus Christ, the righteous. When we turn our eyes toward Christ for a lesson of kingdom living, we catch an eyeful of gentleness.

Of course, there were moments and scenes within Jesus's earthly ministry in which he demonstrates ferocious force and even acts out in righteous anger. It would be insufficient to articulate an understanding of Jesus's actions that operated *only* in gentleness. However, when we examine Jesus's actions and words, we see that his mode of operation among the people around him was gentleness and kindness.

In fact, Jesus himself, when discussing *his heart*—his very being and the inner workings of his soul—said in Matthew, "Take my yoke upon you, and learn from me, *for I am gentle and lowly in heart,* and you will find rest for your souls" (Matt. 11:29 ESV, emphasis added). Commenting on this astonishing verse, Dane Ortlund said:

> In the one place in the Bible (Matt. 11:28–30) where the Son of God pulls back the veil and lets us peer way down into the core of who he is, we are not told that he is "austere and demanding in heart." We are not told that he is "exalted and dignified in heart." We are not even told that he is "joyful and generous in heart." Letting Jesus set the terms, his surprising claim is that he is "gentle and lowly in heart."[2]

Exploring the glory of Jesus's gentleness becomes all the more majestic when we remind ourselves that this Jesus was not only truly man but also truly God. Remember, the one who announces that his heart is "gentle and lowly" is the same one who at that moment was upholding "all things by his powerful word" (Heb. 1:3). If there was ever a person who could have won the day by virtue of forceful power, it was Jesus. Yet he let his ministry be defined by gentleness.

We learn from observing Jesus's ministry on earth that in the kingdom of God we need not juxtapose *power* and *gentleness*; indeed there is power *in* gentleness. Think for a moment about the cosmic consequences that came with Jesus's coming to earth in the first place. We read in Matthew and Luke about the birth of Jesus, and what becomes immediately apparent is that his birth was anything but mighty (Matt. 1:18–25; Luke 2:1–15). Jesus was born to meager parents—Joseph and Mary—in a meager town—Galilee of Nazareth—in meager circumstances—outside the inn—and put into a manger. Nothing about this birth story screams, *"I have come to change the world, and nothing will be the same after my arrival today,"* but that is exactly what transpired.

Jesus came to save Israel not clad in knight's armor on horseback with an army. He came not as a powerful man, muscular and brawny. He came not with a sword and shouts. Jesus came as a helpless Babe. The King of the cosmos, lying in a manger—this story begins in gentleness.

Jesus carried his gentleness with him to his death. After years of showing his "gentle and lowly" heart on earth, Jesus was nailed to a Roman cross as a traitor. Suffering the gruesome and inhumane fate that is Roman crucifixion, Jesus's gentleness was still intact. When he was hung on that tree, "no deceit was found in his mouth" (1 Pet. 2:22), and when he was reviled, "he did not insult in return" (1 Pet. 2:23). When the nails were driven into Jesus's hands and feet, when his side was pierced, he was—at that very moment—upholding the structural integrity of the nails by the word of his power.

At one word, Jesus could have extinguished the tree he hung on and the soldiers who crowned him with thorns. Instead of exercising this right, he went in gentleness.

However, we see the relationship between gentleness and power as we look toward the end of the narrative. What began in gentleness will end in power; this is how it is in the kingdom of God. While the first coming of Jesus was meager and took place in a manger, the second coming of Jesus will be in power and procession. We read in Revelation of the glorious and frightful return of our King:

> Then I saw heaven opened, and there was a white horse. Its rider is called Faithful and True, and with justice he judges and makes war. His eyes were like a fiery flame, and many crowns were on his head. He had a name written that no one knows except himself. He wore a robe dipped in blood, and his name is called the Word of God. The armies that were in heaven followed him on white horses, wearing pure white

> linen. A sharp sword came from his mouth, so that he might strike the nations with it. He will rule them with an iron rod. He will also trample the winepress of the fierce anger of God, the Almighty. And he has a name written on his robe and on his thigh: KING OF KINGS AND LORD OF LORDS. (Rev. 19:11–16)

The theology of the kingdom of God proclaims to an upside-down world that true strength and true power are found in the gentle and meek of this world—it is the gentle Babe of Luke 2 who grows into the powerful King of Revelation 19. But we know on this side of the story that he was conquering the principalities and rulers of the world in both—gentleness and power.

Gentleness of the Tongue, Gentleness of the Temper

What might it look like for us to take the principles of a theologically informed gentleness and apply them to our own lives? What might it look like to live in a way that our actions and words demonstrate that we truly believe there is power and strength in gentleness as shown by our King, Jesus Christ?

Exploring this question, and trying to articulate what a Christian ethic of gentleness might look like in our day-to-day lives, Christopher J. H. Wright once noted:

> Gentleness shows itself when I've learned that the Christlike way to respond to conflicts and quarrels, rejection, unfairness, or harsh words spoken against me, is *not* with bluster and self-defense, *not* with harsh and aggressive words, *not* with angry gestures and facial expressions, *not* with prickles and spikes—but rather, with softness, controlling my tongue and temper.[3]

When I first read Wright's advice here, I found it helpful, but I especially felt myself drawn to those last two categories—the tongue and the temper. Can our theology of the kingdom and the way Jesus turns the world right side up lead to gentleness in our soul, such that we mature enough to have a gentleness of the tongue and a gentleness of the temper?

Gentleness of the Tongue

Being informed by the wisdom of the kingdom, we gain gentleness of the tongue as we come to grips with the reality that it is not the loudest who deserve to be heard. Moreover, wisdom and gentleness of the tongue are not just about volume but love. When we contemplate the truth of theology, it becomes clear that meekness is the way, and we can lay aside our need to be the loudest in the room or the harshest in the room. Instead, wisdom can have its way with our words, and, as we are commanded, we are free to speak "the truth in love" (Eph. 4:15).

The Scriptures have much to say about the life of the tongue in Christian ethics. The biblical writers put much emphasis on this portion of our lives. In the tongue there is much power, and this is a power that can be used for evil or for good.

Consider the third chapter of James, for example. James writes about the tongue as nearly an unconquerable force that can cause destruction beyond repair. He writes:

> Now if we put bits into the mouths of horses so that they obey us, we direct their whole bodies. And consider ships: Though very large and driven by fierce winds, they are guided by a very small rudder wherever the will of the pilot directs. So too, though the tongue is a small part of the body, it boasts great things. Consider how a small fire sets ablaze a large forest. And the tongue is a fire. The tongue, a world of unrighteousness, is placed among our members. It stains the whole body, sets the course of life on fire, and is itself set on fire by hell. Every kind of animal, bird, reptile, and fish is tamed and has been tamed by humankind, but no one can tame the tongue. It is a restless evil, full of deadly poison. With the tongue we bless

> our Lord and Father, and with it we curse people who are made in God's likeness. Blessing and cursing come out of the same mouth. My brothers and sisters, these things should not be this way. Does a spring pour out sweet and bitter water from the same opening? Can a fig tree produce olives, my brothers and sisters, or a grapevine produce figs? Neither can a saltwater spring yield fresh water. (James 3:3–12)

Notice James's comparison to a horse's bit. When a horse rider lays hold of the reins that connect to the bit, he can control the horse and make him go whichever way he chooses. James compares the powerful control of a bit in a horse's mouth to the powerful control the tongue in our mouths has over us. With the tongue we can build up or tear down, we can encourage or belittle, we can praise the Lord, or we can speak in line with the spirit of the age. In short, the life of the tongue is vital within the life of the Christian—our words matter.

James's staggering testimony to the power of the tongue is but one of many passages that speak to how Christians ought to spend their words. Indeed, the Scripture is full of passages pertaining to our speech, and none of it comes close to a command or encouragement to speak harshly or unkindly. On the contrary, the Scriptures consistently communicate that there is wisdom in gentle speech.

Proverbs tells us that "a gentle tongue is a tree of life" (Prov. 15:4 ESV) and that "with patience a ruler may be persuaded, and a soft tongue will break a bone" (Prov. 25:15 ESV). If "the mouth speaks from the overflow of the heart" (Matt. 12:34), then may we be the kind of people filled will stability, wisdom, nuance, and gentleness. If gospel-centered theology can find a home in our heart, then it will be great news to our neighbors that out of the mouth comes that which is in the heart. May we seek the needed discipline of mastering our tongues and working on using this powerful muscle for good. With gentleness, may we cut through the chaos of words flying around today and be a counterexample, showing that "bone-breaking" points can be made with a "soft tongue."

The Digital Tongue

In our day it is not enough to discuss gentleness of merely our physical tongues in our actual speech. In our technologically driven society, much of our "speech" takes place online. The Christian virtue of gentleness of tongue must be applied to our "digital tongue" as well.

It is not difficult to find examples of social media pundits who spend a vast number of words on belittlement and hatred. Sadly, this is true of those who claim the name of Christ as well.

Our digital feeds are filled with sound bites and sentences aimed at self-promotion and the condemnation of others. It is important that we see the terrible reversal of the gospel taking place here. The gospel calls us to make little of ourselves in order that we might make much of God and our neighbors. Many "social media theologians" instead *use* God to make much of themselves as they denigrate their neighbors.

Never has it been easier to get your "voice" in front of others. You are, even at this moment, just a few clicks away from publishing another opinion for the masses to see. Like we do with our physical tongue, we have a choice and an obligation to use our "digital tongue" with gentleness, for the glory of the Lord and the good of our neighbor.

If I can say it frankly, the world is not in need of more hot takes or overly opinionated social media users posting long threads about what is wrong with those around them. We are, however, in major need of Christians using the digital space with wisdom and gentleness. While social media and other digital outlets give us the opportunity to speak with force and add to the cacophony compounding each day, they also afford us the chance to be kind with our words and wise with our speech.

How might the digital communities in which we take part look different if we were actively seeking out chances for kindness or opportunities to be nuanced instead of enraged? It is arguably in the digital sphere where Christians need to take Philippians 4:5 to heart the most. In this passage, Paul commands us, "Let your *reasonableness* be known to everyone. The Lord is at hand" (ESV). In a digital economy of outrage, may we be gentle and nuanced outposts for reasonableness.

Gentleness of the Temper

Beyond the life of our tongue, we ourselves should be defined by gentleness. If the tongue ought to be mastered by gentleness, so should the temper. Between being a theology professor and a local church pastor, my life is often filled with meetings. I have noticed that those I'm most drawn toward in meetings—those whose leadership I find myself wanting to follow—are those with a calm spirit. When the church or institution seems to be in chaos, they seem to be levelheaded. Not because they don't understand the gravity of the situation or the importance of our task but rather because they have an anchored soul that will not allow them to lose their cool. Over years of observing, I have noticed that what I am drawn to in these individuals is their gentleness of temper.

As we did for gentleness of the tongue, any conversation dealing with gentleness of the temper would benefit from looking to Proverbs. In the book of Proverbs, we read that "whoever is slow to anger is better than the mighty, and he who rules his spirit than he who takes a city" (16:32 ESV). There is a reason that among those qualifications listed for those who wish to become a pastor is gentleness. Paul says that elders must be "not a bully but gentle, not quarrelsome" (1 Tim. 3:3). Proverbs and Paul here are getting at the wisdom that is a gentle spirit.

A gentle spirit that manifests itself in gentleness of the temper is not to be confused with weakness. On the contrary, as we've seen how kingdom ethics are often upside down from how our world views things, a gentle spirit is a sign of much power. To have a gentle spirit shows that a person has the power to master much of the inner chaos that weaker individuals let spill out onto others. It takes power not to revile in return when reviled or to threaten in return when suffering; this is the power Christ demonstrated on his way to the cross (1 Pet. 2:23).

If our Lord, Christ himself, declares that his yoke is easy and his heart is gentle, and if he teaches his people that there is much wisdom in a life of gentleness, we ought to listen. We must not fall for the temptation to write off harshness or being quick to anger as a personality trait or a personal preference. Rather, we ought to set our mind's eye on the gentleness shown us by the triune God as he redeemed us even while we were his enemies and seek to internalize that gentleness and be marked by it.

Chapter Ten

Self-Control

Whenever I am tempted, whenever clouds
  arise,
When songs give place to sighing, when
  hope within me dies,
I draw the closer to Him, from care He sets
  me free;
His eye is on the sparrow, and I know He
  watches me;
His eye is on the sparrow, and I know He
  watches me.[1]

At the turn of the twentieth century, poet Civilla Martin penned these lines after visiting with a friend who was dealing with a sickness of some significance. After asking her friend how she remained in such joy after years of unrelenting sickness, the friend famously replied, "His eye is on the sparrow, and I know he watches over me." Martin thought there was power in the simplicity of the statement, and meditating on it, she wrote her well-known hymn, "His Eye Is on the Sparrow."

For inspiration, Martin pulled from Jesus's words in Matthew 10: "Aren't two sparrows sold for a penny? Yet not one of them falls to the ground without your Father's consent. But even the hairs of your head have all been counted. So don't be afraid; you are worth more than many sparrows" (vv. 29–31).

As it was the inspiration for a century-old hymn, this passage has inspired generations of Christians, and for good reason. In the third century, theologian and one of the church's most famous preachers, John Chrysostom, reflected on this passage, saying, "He is not ignorant of anything that befalls us, and loves us more truly than a father, and so loves us, as to have numbered our very hairs; we ought not to be afraid."[2]

Whether from Civilla Martin in the twentieth century or John Chrysostom in the fourth century, and countless Christians in between, the message of Matthew 10 has comforted countless Christians with the news that God *has us*. There is not a corner of the universe to which God's hand does not stretch. There is not a crevasse in the cosmos that is not under God's watchful gaze. There is not a blade of grass or grain of sand outside of God's knowledge. God is the God over all, and his sovereignty and reign know no bounds.

As the Dutch theologian, Abraham Kuyper, once stated, "There is not a square inch in the whole domain of our human existence over which Christ, who is Sovereign overall, does not cry, 'Mine!'"[3]

In theology we have two terms to help us describe this great grandeur of God: *sovereignty* and *providence*. Sovereignty gets at God's authority and reign over all things, while providence describes his care and control over the happenings of our world. From God's kind providence we receive his many good gifts, and out of that same providence God takes from us as well. While God's providence, from our perspective, can be both sweet and bitter, we know it is *always* good.

The oft-quoted passage of Romans 8:28 tells us, "We know that all things work together for the good of those who love God, who are called according to his purpose." So, even when providence tastes a touch bitter, it is nevertheless good, as it comes from our good God.

One passage of Scripture that illuminates and informs regarding God's good providence is worth quoting at length. It comes again from Matthew. The apostle records Jesus's words and with them hopes to show Christians that in the providential care of the Lord, they need not be anxious. Jesus says:

> Therefore I tell you: Don't worry about your life, what you will eat or what you will drink; or about your body, what you will wear. Isn't life more than food and the body more than clothing? Consider the birds of the sky:

> They don't sow or reap or gather into barns, yet your heavenly Father feeds them. Aren't you worth more than they? Can any of you add one moment to his life span by worrying? And why do you worry about clothes? Observe how the wildflowers of the field grow: They don't labor or spin thread. Yet I tell you that not even Solomon in all his splendor was adorned like one of these. If that's how God clothes the grass of the field, which is here today and thrown into the furnace tomorrow, won't he do much more for you—you of little faith? So don't worry, saying, "What will we eat?" or "What will we drink?" or "What will we wear?" For the Gentiles eagerly seek all these things, and your heavenly Father knows that you need them. But seek first the kingdom of God and his righteousness, and all these things will be provided for you. (Matt. 6:25–33)

God has his eye on every sparrow and clothes every lily of the field. He cares for this world and those who inhabit it. In his providential care, he rains down love on those he created. The Scriptures' use of seemingly small and insignificant subjects like sparrows and lilies show that God knows and cares about even the smallest of details in our lives, and even these are not outside of his control.

Divine Providence and Self-Control

One only need look at the major arc of the narrative of Scripture to see God's providence written all over it. Time and again, the Lord sovereignly guides Israel, sovereignly provides for Israel, and sovereignly preserves Israel. Apart from God's divine providence, Israel would have succumbed to destruction at several turns in this grand story. But beyond the grand narrative of Scripture's story line, God's providence unfolds in individual passages as well. In the book of Proverbs, for example, we read that God controls the hearts of kings like a stream of water in his hands and he is able to turn even the mightiest leaders wherever he wills (Prov. 21:1). Or, as another Proverb informs us, it is not only the kings' paths he has providence over but also ours. Proverbs 16:9 informs us that while our hearts plan our own ways, it is really the Lord who establishes our steps.

The truth of divine providence in Christian theology is both gorgeous and glorious, but what might this doctrine have to do with the virtue of self-control? You might think this doctrine is an unlikely candidate to inform our self-control. After all, if providence and sovereignty are about *God's* control, how could they inform *our* self-control? Isn't self-control about trying harder and white-knuckling it, rather than just trusting in God's sovereignty and providence?

God's control has much to do with self-control, as our ability to trust in God's providential care demonstrates how much we agree or disagree with the psalmist when he writes:

> LORD, you are my portion and my cup of
>   blessing;
> you hold my future.
> The boundary lines have fallen for me in
>   pleasant places;
> indeed, I have a beautiful inheritance.
> (Ps. 16:5–6)

God's providence frees us to pursue self-control. For God has made our "lines" fall in pleasant places, and like the sparrows in the sky, he watches over us. If we were left to fend for ourselves and if we had no gracious Father to take care of our needs, self-indulgence might be necessary. When we dive into self-indulgence, we show that we do not trust God's providential care, and think rather that we must fend for ourselves. For example:

- If we are wronged by someone and are self-indulgent with harsh words in retaliation in hopes to avenge ourselves, we show that we do not trust in God's providential care as he said, "Vengeance is mine" (Deut. 32:35; Rom. 12:19).
- If we have lustful eyes and become self-indulgent in sexual immorality, we show that we do not trust God's providential

care in giving the good gift of sexuality between man and wife (Prov. 5:18–19; Heb. 13:4).

- If we are eager for the applause of man and are self-indulgent with attention and seek to leverage our own talents for the admiration of our peers or for building our "brand," we prove that we do not trust God's providential care in wrapping our identity in the identity of his Son, Jesus Christ (2 Cor. 5:17; Gal. 2:20).

We can be self-indulgent in a host of ways—words, thoughts, laziness, food, sexuality, time, entertainment, etc. Each of these is an avenue for a lack of self-control, which demonstrates our distrust in the good God who takes care of us in his providence. Yet we can practice restraint and the wisdom of a controlled appetite and desires because we know that God will providentially take care of our needs. To see how a robust doctrine of divine providence might aid our efforts toward self-control, it will help to look a little more at what the Scripture has to say about self-control as a fruit of the Spirit.

A Biblical Understanding of Self-Control

As we have seen with the previous virtues that comprise the fruit of the Spirit, the Scripture has much to say about this final fruit. In the Scriptures, self-control is tied closely with having wisdom. It is wise for us to develop the ability to be in control of ourselves so that when we are presented options that appeal to our desires and appetites, we can choose those which lead to life and not death. Proverbs tells us that "a person who does not control his temper is like a city whose wall is broken down" (Prov. 25:28). Self-control acts as a barrier to defend our body and soul from that which will harm us and others. A life of self-indulgence is a city without walls into which evil and destruction have free range.

Self-control plays an important role in Paul's list of the fruit of the Spirit in Galatians 5:22–23. The previous eight virtues are things to be pursued—we are to actively *go after* love, joy, peace, kindness, goodness, gentleness, and faithfulness. Self-control, however, acts in a more defensive manner; instead of going after this particular virtue, self-control prevents us from going after a host of life-ruining vices.

This is likely one reason Paul put self-control as the final fruit in his list. Self-control is to act as the counterbalance for all the final vices listed in the "works of the flesh," also in Galatians 5. If you will recall our comparative table in chapter 1, you will remember that while only nine virtues make up the fruit of the Spirit, sixteen vices are listed in the works of the flesh. While we will not relist all sixteen here, some of the works of the flesh are sexual immorality, impurity, idolatry, jealousy, fits of anger, envy, and drunkenness.

The wisdom that is self-control is revealed in the fact that in this one fruit of the Spirit you can prevent your life from running down any of these treacherous paths.

Paul's letter to Titus picks up on this concept of the self-controlled life being a life of wisdom that prevents all kinds of evil in our lives. Paul writes to Titus:

> For the grace of God has appeared, bringing salvation for all people, instructing us to deny godlessness and worldly lusts and to live in a sensible, righteous, and godly way in the present age, while we wait for the blessed hope, the appearing of the glory of our great God and Savior, Jesus Christ. He gave himself for us to redeem us from all lawlessness and to cleanse for himself a people for his own possession, eager to do good works. (Titus 2:11–14)

We see in Paul's words here that the gospel of Jesus Christ, which brings salvation to all people, trains us to "deny godlessness and worldly lusts." How does the gospel prevent us from these two evils? It does so by instilling self-control in our lives. And by our self-control, we possess the wisdom to choose that which will bring life to ourselves and glory to our God instead of that which will bring destruction to ourselves and glory to the prince of darkness.

Wise Living under the Care of Providence

To live a life of self-control is to live a life of wisdom. However, given that this chapter argues for the benefits of Christian theology on the path to self-control, it is important to note here that theology is not enough. While Christian theology is a *necessary* ingredient to develop a life of self-control, it is not a *sufficient* one. (In fact, this is true of theology's relationship to all of the fruit of the Spirit!)

Just think of the many Christian leaders in our day who have had a robust and proper theology working in their lives who still, tragically, had a moral or ministerial failure that led to public shame on Christ's church and their disqualification from ministry. Theology, on its own, will not equip you with sufficient self-control to prevent a bad decision that would do serious harm to both your life and your witness for the gospel.

While theology alone is not sufficient to deliver you to a life full of self-control, it is, nevertheless, a grace-filled aid in the journey. What's more, the doctrine of divine providence is but one of many you could have in your tool kit in building a foundation of self-control. What Christian theology teaches about God's love, God's judgment, God's church, God's sanctifying work, and of course, God's gospel can all advance our journey toward self-control. Each of these beautiful truths in the system of Christian theology, and many more like them, can come together to forge a path that leads God's children toward the wise life of self-control.

Self-indulgence is easy; self-control is a daily struggle. However, the Scriptures show us that this is a struggle worth undertaking. While indulging in whatever passions and pleasures grab our mind's eye may bring satisfaction for a moment, we know this is a vapor. It will leave us unsatisfied still and longing for something more. The fruit that falls from the tree of self-indulgence is poisoned. While it looks fine to eat, it takes hold of us and brings chaos into our lives.

There is a better way. A life characterized by self-control, while hard to maintain, is a life characterized by stability and wisdom. Moreover, a life characterized by wise self-control under the care of divine providence leads to real, lasting joy. Remember, God has made our lines fall in pleasant places (Ps. 16:5–6). At the right hand of God are pleasures forevermore (Ps. 16:11). While self-indulgence brings a fleeting joy that comes and goes in a second, wise self-control brings about an eternal joy that will last "forevermore."

Bring your mind back to Jesus's glorious words to the Samaritan woman at the well: in our Lord we find the true living water. He is the water from which those who drink will never be thirsty again. Self-indulgence will give you a taste of pleasure, which vanishes and needs to be replenished over and over. In this way, self-indulgence makes you a slave for the next taste. Yet, when we live a self-controlled life of wisdom and trust Jesus that in him there is living water that will satisfy our souls, we may rest.

Conclusion

Strong in Mind, Gentle in Sprit: Theology for the Glory of God and the Good of Others

We come now to the close of our time considering how the life of the mind should lead to the life of the soul. What is hopefully apparent by this point is that sustained contemplation of the grandeur and grace of our God should lead to the development of the fruit of the Spirit in our lives. The life of our mind is immediately connected to the life of our hearts and the life of our hands.

There is much we could say in conclusion to the many doctrines and many fruit of the Spirit we have examined. However, three brief passages from the apostle Paul will aid us as we close. The three passages are Philippians 4:8; Romans 12:2; and 2 Corinthians 3:18. In these three passages, Paul helps us by making explicit the vital connection between the life of the mind and the life of the soul. We can summarize these three passages, bringing them all together in once sentence: *Contemplate the good, the true, and the beautiful in Christ, and in so doing be transformed by the renewing of your mind by beholding Christ from one degree of glory to another.* Or, to use Paul's words: "Think about these things" and "be transformed" by "beholding."

Think about These Things (Phil. 4:8)

You possess something of immense value—your attention. The world wants it, and it will throw much at you to get it. There are folks whose primary job is to continually maintain and upgrade sophisticated algorithms to guarantee that your attention will stay fixed on your phone. Neil Postman was correct in his incredibly insightful book, *Amusing Ourselves to Death,* when he warned that we are people in danger of simply becoming an audience.[1] The world is a stage where your gaze and attention are the commodity.

For this reason and countless others, Paul's conclusion to his letter to the Philippians is just as relevant today as it was in first-century Philippi. Concluding his letter, Paul instructs the saints at Philippi, saying, "Finally brothers and sisters, whatever is true, whatever is honorable, whatever is just, whatever is pure, whatever is lovely, whatever is commendable—if there is any moral excellence and if there is anything praiseworthy—*dwell on these things*" (Phil. 4:8, emphasis added).

What Paul understood, and what we must understand, is that whatever we give our attention to *will form us as people.* If our minds stay on the ever-changing and increasingly shallow events of our culture, we will continue to decline in our wisdom and reasonableness as followers of Christ. However, if we let Paul's command sink into our lives and have the self-control to look up and out of the dizzying array of distractions surrounding us, giving instead a hard, sustained look at that which is good, true, and beautiful, we may be transformed into wise and stable men and women.

Be Transformed (Rom. 12:2)

Paul's letter to the Philippians was not the only place where he made clear the connection between our thought life and our actions. In his epistle to the Romans, Paul writes: "Do not be conformed to this age, but *be transformed by the renewing of your mind,* so that you may discern what is the good, pleasing, and perfect will of God" (Rom. 12:2, emphasis added).

Maybe no verse gets at the heart of this book like Romans 12:2. Renewing our minds has the power to *transform* us that we might be wise and able to discern the will of God, finding what is good and perfect.

It is sad that in our day theology often receives the caricature of being obsolete. Some discuss theology as if it is a pastime for those who are out of touch, an irrelevant exercise providing nothing more than intellectual stimulation.

Hopefully, the previous ten chapters help lay to rest this falsity about theology, but if they do not, Paul's words here to the church in Rome should.

Contemplating God in Christian theology is no mere intellectualism. On the contrary, setting our mind on God and all things in relation to God allows us to gaze at him who is love. In so doing, we will be transformed by the renewal of our minds. A mind full of truth should lead to a heart full of love and hands full of care.

Behold the Glory of the Lord (2 Cor. 3:18)

The final passage of our three, 2 Corinthians 3:18, is one of my personal favorites. In this glorious chapter, Paul contrasts the saints of the old covenant and those of the new. He recalls the scene we discussed earlier in the book in which Moses, after seeing the goodness of the Lord in Exodus 33, comes down from Mount Sinai with his face veiled so that he might not startle the other Israelites. Paul says that reading the old covenant is like attempting to look at God through a veil, like Moses. On the contrary, seeing God in the face of Jesus Christ is like seeing God with the veil removed so that we can behold his beauty and splendor uninhibited.

Paul writes, "And we all, with unveiled faces, *beholding the glory of the Lord, are being transformed in the same image from one degree of glory to another*. For this comes from the Lord who is the Spirit" (2 Cor. 3:18, emphasis added).

It is easy to miss Paul's progression here, but it is important for us to see his argument unfold. Working backwards through this verse helps the meaning come forward:

1. The Holy Spirit ministers to us by giving us,
2. The grace to move from one degree of glory to another,
3. Until we are transformed into the same glorious image of Jesus Christ,
4. Which occurs as we behold his glory.

This passage is brimming with beauty. While we have seen throughout this book that Christian theology has a considerable number of practical benefits, one of the greatest is simply *beholding the glory of God*. One of the most practical things you can do in your life—counter to the idea that theology is an irrelevant ivory-tower pastime—is catch an eyeful of God's grandeur and grace. While we should always attempt to work out our theology and ask important questions like "How can I *live* this truth out today?" we should not forget that there is immense wisdom in simply beholding this great God of ours. When we behold him, we begin to look like him, as we are transformed from one degree of glory to another.

Against Such Things There Is No Law

In examining how the life of the mind can and should lead to the life of the soul, the fruit of the Spirit in Galatians 5:22–23 has been our compass, pointing to the true north of wisdom and worship. There is, however, an important clause in this section of Scripture that we have yet to discuss.

Paul brings his section on the fruit of the Spirit to a close by saying, "The law is not against such things." While countless laws against those vices make up the works of the flesh in Galatians 5—things like idolatry, enmity, strife, jealousy, fits of anger, dissensions, divisions, and envy—there is *no such law* against practicing those virtues that make up the fruit of the Spirit: love, joy, peace, patience, kindness, goodness, faithfulness, gentleness, and self-control.

If you feel the need to indulge, indulge in the fruit of the Spirit. We *ought* to indulge in kindness, indulge in love, and indulge in gentleness. We can come to drink from the fountain of peace and patience and know it is impossible to drink too much. This fruit—for remember that the "fruits" of the Spirit are really one "fruit"—ought to infect every area of our lives. Not only the life of our minds but our relationships, our emotions, our vocations, our passions, our thoughts, our words, our deeds—everything about us should be marked by these virtues, for "against such things there is no law."

As we saw in chapter 1, and as we see in Galatians 5, the proper end of the fruit of the Spirit is that we love one another and bear one another's burdens (Gal. 5:14; 6:2). We ought, then, to indulge in each item of the list.

A Final Exhortation and Hope

I'm aware that this book will not change the overheated discourse of many theological discussions today. I'm aware that this book will not tear down the four "problems with theology" listed in chapter 1. I'm aware that these pages might not offer a satisfactory answer for those who assume the caricature of theological contemplation that it is merely a venue of arrogance and bears no real significance for how we live our lives. However, while this book will not answer every gripe against Christian theology, I hope, at least for you, reader, it might help move your theological journey a few steps closer toward the destination of the fruit of the Spirit.

In all of our thinking about God, we have a choice. We can be characterized by the "works of the flesh," so that theology leads us to devour one another. Or we can insist that casting our intellectual gaze on God will instead be marked by the fruit of the Spirit and will lead not to devouring one another but to bearing one another's burdens. This is the way forward for Christian theology. From the greatest vocational theologian to the newest believer who is for the first time thinking about God and his world, may we all find that the life of our minds leads to the life of our souls.

Throughout these pages we have discussed the nine virtues that make up the fruit of the Spirit and examined each one through a number of theological realities. We have covered Christian doctrines such as divine simplicity, the kingdom of God, union with Christ, justification, the atonement, the doctrine of creation, imputed righteousness, providence, and more. In each of these discussions, the hope is not merely to grow in knowledge and understanding but to demonstrate how the theological life can transform us into a people marked by the fruit of the Spirit. Therefore, in coming to the final pages of our study, it is appropriate to close with a final exhortation and hope for all our pursuit of Christian theology.

May our theology lead to love. As we set our minds on the God who doesn't merely *have love* but who *is himself love,* may our contemplation of his glory and grace transform us into people who are marked by love. May our lives be spent in a threefold love in which we love the Lord, love our neighbor, and have a healthy sense of loving ourselves. In love, may we count others as more significant than ourselves and pour ourselves out for their good. May theological truth melt our hard hearts, and in the ashes of indifference may the buds of affection and adoration sprout. May our theology lead to love.

May our theology lead to joy. May the product of the thousand gears of truth that turn in Christian theology be to the production of unshakable joy in our souls. May our joy be rooted in something more everlasting than our fleeting feeling or preferences; on the contrary, may we insist that our joy be as unchanging as our God. While the world feels ever ill and as our culture continues to decay around us, may we not be caught in shifting sand but standing firm in the truth about God and all things in relation to God. May our theology lead to joy.

May our theology lead to peace. While the world seems committed to biting and devouring one another, may the truths that have gloriously infected us down to our bones find a better way. May division and discord find a foe in our lives. May the us-versus-them spirit of our age be uprooted in our hearts and replaced with a recognition of the image of God even in those we disagree with most vehemently. May the peace of God rule our hearts such that every other swaying emotion is put under the reign of the deep peace that could only come from a lifetime of gazing at God's glory. May our theology lead to peace.

May our theology lead to patience. Instead of demanding that life move at our preferred speed, may we develop the countercultural ability to be still and patient. May our reflection on the deep things of God instruct us in stillness and dependence on the Lord to reveal himself. May we abandon the delusion that we can master our time and instead revel in the Lord's sovereign reign over every minute of our existence. May we receive each second as grace and resolve that levelheaded reasonableness will be our method of existence. As we contemplate God and all things in relation to God, may we walk away from the lifelong journey with an increasing sense of the "awe of Moses and the limp of Jacob." May our theology lead to patience.

May our theology lead to kindness. Ours is a day short on kindness. The spirit of the age is one in which those who stand on the other side of the political or denominational aisle from us are cut down and mocked. Arguments and nuance have given way to scoffing and sarcasm. May our theology lead us to swim upstream from a culture bent on belittlement. On the contrary, may our love of God's truth color our actions, thoughts, and words with kindness. May we be a people known for extending kindness in a world in which it is hard to find. May we live with resolved convictions that need not shake even in the strongest winds, but may we hold them with winsome kindness. May our theology lead to kindness.

May our theology lead to goodness. May our investing our thought life in the good, the true, and the beautiful manifest in our day-to-day life demonstrating the good, the true, and the beautiful. May our theology of a good God and his good world transform our hearts such that we put our hands to the plow and build that which is good. May our striving for goodness not grow weary, and may we be zealous for goodness in our day. May our love and pursuit of goodness both in personal and social realms allow for justice to roll down. May our theology lead to goodness.

May our theology lead to faithfulness. In our hours of contemplation and pages read, may we find reason after reason to remain steadfast and faithful. May we have the long game in mind with Christian faithfulness and pursue that which will last—God's glory and his kingdom. May our excuses, shortcuts, sinfulness, crippling doubt, and fickleness find a swift death in theologically induced faithfulness. May our theology lead some of us into faithfulness on the mission field, faithfulness as a mother, faithfulness as a father, faithfulness as an employee, faithfulness in leading, and faithfulness in following. May our hearts be softened and our knees be strengthened by contemplating grandeur and grace of our God. May our theology lead to faithfulness.

May our theology lead to gentleness. As we follow the upside-down pattern of our King and his kingdom, may our theology allow us to see that real might is found not in vengeance or self-seeking but in gentleness. May gentleness season both our tongue and our temper. In a culture whose words are mingled with cynicism, sarcasm, anger, contention, and self-promotion, may our tongue be conquered by gentleness leading to speech seasoned with love. May our theology develop in us a gentle spirit in which we will find real purpose and power. May our theology lead to gentleness.

May our theology lead to self-control. May our theology lead to the kind of wisdom that knows life and death are in God's hands, and we need not worry that we will lack any good thing from his hand. May the high stakes of obedience lead to a self-control which protects and preserves us against the prince of darkness and anything that might pull us away from the path of obedience. May our theological contemplation come down from the abstract in a way that leads to self-awareness, and may we all be in tune with our feelings, emotions, passions, temptations, affection, and the like such that we can live controlled and stable lives. May our theological contemplation aid in convincing us that a life of self-controlled righteousness under God's providential care is worth a thousand lives of sinful self-indulgence.

May we have strong minds and gentle spirits that seek to use Christian theology for the glory of God and the good of others. May the task of Christian theology give us even a small taste of heaven on earth as we join in that eternal joy of gazing upon the glory of our Lord. May our theology be the death of the works of the flesh and the manifestation of the fruit of the Spirit in our lives. May the life of the mind lead to the life of the soul in all of us as we spend our days contemplating God and all things in relation to God.

Appendix

I'm New to Theology, Where Do I Start?

The first sentence of this book is a quote from a theologian named John Webster: "Theology is the study of God and all things in relation to God." This definition is important, for it shows readers that theology is a God-centered activity. However, Webster has another quote that is important for getting started in Christian theology. He writes:

> Christian theology is biblical reasoning. It is an activity of the created intellect, judged, reconciled, redeemed and sanctified through the works of the Son and the Spirit. More closely, Christian theology is part of reason's answer to the divine Word which addresses creatures through the intelligible service of the prophets and apostles. It has its origin in the Spirit-sustained hearing of the divine Word; it is rational contemplation

> and articulation of God's communicative presence.[1]

This quote is helpful to new (and seasoned) theologians for a few reasons:

1. It reminds us that Christian theology is a Christian task. We need the Spirit's guidance and conviction. We need the Trinity's accommodating word and revelation. We need the Son to redeem our soul. Christian theology with an unbelieving heart can lead to devastating places. So the first step of Christian theology is to trust and follow the God of Christian theology.
2. Christian theology is only possible because God actually wants to be known. As Webster notes, God has revealed himself to us through the intelligible service of the prophets and apostles. The Scripture is our theological foundation and our ultimate authority. The Christian theologian must be a lover of books but must also with great passion love *the* book.
3. Finally, Webster's quote shows us that Christian theology isn't merely summarizing; it's active reasoning. While our

> final authority is the Bible, we recruit the help of church history, philosophy, great literature, nature, and the like to reason toward the glory of God and the good of others. We're the inheritors of thousands of years of conversation surrounding Christ, and we should steward that gift well.

Moving beyond Webster's helpful quote in getting us started with Christian theology, here are a few more pointers for getting started:

1. *You should do theology in a local church.* Theology is not a lone-wolf adventure, and theology done wrong can lead to destruction. This is a glorious but weighty enterprise so you should do your theology in the context of those who have covenanted to watching your soul.
2. *You should recognize that there are different kinds of theology.* Like most projects, you need multiple tools to get the job done. Theology is similar. For example, while the word *theology* can be used to describe the study of God and all things in relation to God, you can go about that activity in multiple

ways. Often, theologians categorize theology in four separate disciplines:

Biblical Theology	What does the Bible, or a portion of the Bible, say about a topic?
Historical Theology	What did certain eras of Christians think about a topic?
Philosophical Theology	Do my conclusions about this topic make logical sense?
Systematic Theology	How do my conclusions about this topic impact other doctrines in the Christian faith, and how do I contemplate and construct from this topic?

Keeping these categories in mind will help you use the right tool when a question arises as you study the Lord.

3. *Study and read from different eras of church history.* Jesus declared that not even the gates of hell would prevail against his church. One sign of that promise is the reality that while many threats have come up against the church, especially theological threats, the Lord has used different eras of Christians to maintain and protect the truth. Reading from each era will help

you be a well-rounded theologian and have a deep appreciation for the great tradition. For example, the table below shows different eras of church history and the area of theology they spent much time and ink defending:

Early Church / Patristic Era	Christology / Trinitarianism
Medieval Theologians	The Doctrine of God / Theology Proper
Reformation Theologians	The Doctrine of Salvation / Scripture
Post-Reformation Theologians	Prolegomena / Theological Method
Modern-Era Theologians	The Doctrine of Scripture / Mankind

4. *Remember theological method.* Theology is both a science and an art. Therefore, there is no magic formula in which you can input a question and it goes through the process just to pop out the other side a well-formulated theological concept. Instead, theology is a great practice that intermingles both scientific processes and artistry. However, there is typically a method to theology. While you'll find many differing

theological methods and while none of these methods are a silver bullet, below is a good pattern to follow for those beginning theology:

Step One: Pray	Christian theology is a Christian practice, so start with the source. Beg the Lord to give you wisdom and insight.
Step Two: Exegesis	Work through pertinent passages that deal with the topic you are thinking about. Think through each part of Scripture; then ask how the parts connect to the whole of Scripture.
Step Three: Biblical Theology	See above. In biblical theology, you should concern yourself with what the entirety of the Bible says about a topic or what a portion of the Bible says about a topic, or the way a topic progresses.
Step Four: Historical Theology	Typically, in a two-thousand-year-old faith, being novel is not a good thing. Once you think you have a theological idea, test it against the creeds, confessions, and confessors of the great tradition. History can act as a guide rail to keep you on the path of the faith once and for all delivered to the saints.

Step Five: Philosophical Theology	Steps four and five are rather interchangeable; however, in this step, you want to make sure that your premises logically lead to your conclusions. Make sure you have epistemological (study of knowledge) authority and validation to say what you're thinking.
Step Six: Systematic Theology	God is a God of unity, not disorder. Therefore, typically the affirmation or denial of any doctrine is an affirmation or denial of a few other doctrines. Find the systematic relationships between doctrines. Also ask what constructive and contemplative difference each doctrine makes in your Christian life and dogma.
Step Seven: Begin Again	Theology is a lifelong process. Moreover, we should not pretend that we come to the biblical data as a "blank slate." Instead, we come to the biblical text with our theology in hand knowing Christian theology will help prevent us from bad interpretation. We begin the process again, over and over, as the Lord conforms us from one degree of glory to the next as we behold him.

5. *Remember theology is a lifelong process.* The final point in the chart above

is worth its own section. Many times in the life of a theologian, you will feel frustrated at simply not understanding. Its important to remember what you're attempting to do in these moments: you, a finite creature, are attempting to think about and articulate the infinite God of the universe who told the stars where to hang and the ocean where to stop. This is a *difficult task*. It's okay if it does not come easy. Rest assured that in those days when you are wrestling with theological truths the Lord is actually working on you *in those moments.* It's not just in the conclusions of theology that we are sanctified but also in the wrestling with theology.

6. *Finally, be a reader.* You'll find that the best theologians are often the theologians who read other voices. The Lord has been kind in letting us do theology in community, and through the gift of books, we can read and heed what other Christian thinkers have said. Here are a few books to help you get started if you're new to theology:

    Knowing God and *Concise Theology* by J. I. Packer

The Little Book for New Theologians by Kelly Kapic

The Trinity by Scott Swain

Plain Theology for Plain People by Charles Octavius Boothe

None Greater by Matthew Barrett

Taking God at His Word by Kevin DeYoung

Women of the Word and *None Like Him* by Jen Wilkin

Everyone Is a Theologian by R. C. Sproul

On the Incarnation by Athanasius

Everyday Theology by Mary Wiley

Delighting in the Trinity by Michael Reeves

Knowledge of the Holy by A. W. Tozer

The Christian's Reasonable Service by Wilhelmus à Brakel (*multivolume, tougher read than the others but still a good guide*)

7. For those a little more seasoned in theological studies, or those who have

worked through many of the above, here are a few further recommendations:

- *Theoretical-Practical Theology* by Petrus Van Mastricht
- *Reformed Dogmatics* by Herman Bavinck
- *The Major Works* by Anselm
- *Summa Theologica* by Thomas Aquinas
- *God without Measure* by John Webster
- *The Lord Is Good* by Christopher Holmes
- *On God and Christ* by Gregory of Nazianzus
- *Drama of Doctrine* by Kevin Vanhoozer
- *The Institutes of the Christian Religion* by John Calvin
- *On the Trinity* by Hillary of Poitiers
- *City of God* and *The Trinity* by Augustine

Notes

Chapter 1: Why Do the Theologians Rage?

1. While this definition of theology comes from many sources, in my theological development I was first made aware of its importance from John Webster. John Webster, *God without Measure,* vol. 1 (London: T&T Clarke, 2016), 1.

2. Augustine, *The Trinity,* ed. H. Dressler, trans. S. McKenna (Washington: CUA Press, 1963), 26.

3. Jen Wilkin, *Women of the Word: How to Study the Bible with Both Our Hearts and Our Minds* (Wheaton: Crossway, 2014), 33.

4. Thomas Aquinas, *Commentary on the Sentences,* Bk. 1, dist. 2, exposition of the text. Quoted in Giles Emery, *The Trinity: An Introduction to Catholic Doctrine on the Triune God* (Washington: CUA Press, 2011), xiii. Both quotes, from Augustine and Aquinas, I first came across in Giles Emery's excellent (but academic) book on the Trinity.

Chapter 2: Love

1. Charles Spurgeon, "The First Fruit of the Spirit," in *Metropolitan Tabernacle Pulpit,* vol. 30, 289–300.

2. Anselm, "Proslogion" in *The Major Works,* ed. Brian Davies and G. R. Evans (Oxford: Oxford University Press, 1998), 87.

3. Charles Spurgeon, "The Condescension of Christ" in *New Park Street Pulpit,* vol. 3, 349–56.

4. "The Creed of Nicaea" in Henry Bettenson and Chris Maunder, ed. *Documents of the Christian Church,* 4th ed. (Oxford: Oxford University Press, 2011), 26–28.

5. C. S. Lewis, *The Four Loves* (New York: Harper Collins, 1960), 155–56.

Chapter 3: Joy

1. John Piper, *Desiring God: Meditations of a Christian Hedonist* (Colorado Springs: Multnomah, 2011), 18.

2. Aaron Menikoff, *Character Matters: Shepherding in the Fruit of the Spirit* (Chicago: Moody, 2020), 42–44.

3. C. S. Lewis, "Introduction" to Athanasius, *On the Incarnation* (New York: St. Vladimir's Seminary Press, 2011), 13.

4. This alliteration concerning God's immutability is from my forthcoming book: Ronni Kurtz, *No Shadow of Turning: Divine Immutability in the Economy of Redemption* (Fearn, Ross-Shire, UK: Christian Focus, forthcoming). Augustine has a great section relating our joy to God's unchanging nature. See Augustine, *Letter to Dioscorus* in *Nicene and Post-Nicene Fathers,* volume 1, 443.

5. Steve Kroft, Interview with Tom Brady, *60 Minutes,* CBS, June 2005.

6. C. S. Lewis, *Mere Christianity* (New York: Harper One, 2015) 137.

Chapter 4: Peace

1. I'm grateful to Aaron Menikoff for making this great observation. See Menikoff, *Character Matters,* 56.

2. Augustine, *Confessions* (Oxford: Oxford University Press, 2008), 3.

3. "The Creed of Nicaea" *Documents of the Christian Church,* 26–28.

Chapter 5: Patience

1. Matthew Levering, *Scripture and Metaphysics: Aquinas and the Renewal of Trinitarian Theology* (Malden: Blackwell Publishing, 2004), 3.

Chapter 6: Kindness

1. Douglas Moo, *Galatians in Baker Exegetical Commentary of the New Testament* (Grand Rapids: Baker Academic, 2013), 264.

2. Russell Moore, *Onward: Engaging the Culture without Losing the Gospel* (Nashville: B&H, 2015), 187–205.

3. Moore, *Onward,* 200.

Chapter 7: Goodness

1. C. S. Lewis, *The Magician's Nephew* (New York: Scholastic, 1955), 116.

2. One theologian, Christopher R. J. Holmes, has written a splendid book covering the theology of God's goodness by examining the Psalms in search of a robust doctrine of the perfection of divine goodness. Holmes says that "goodness has a scriptural density and range that even the other great

attribute—love—does not quite have." In short, God's goodness is all over the Scriptures. Christopher R. J. Holmes, *The Lord Is Good* (Downers Grove, IL: IVP Academic, 2018).

3. Holmes, *The Lord Is Good,* 181.

Chapter 8: Faithfulness

1. J. I. Packer, *Knowing God* (Downers Grove, IL: InterVarsity Press, 1993), 64.

Chapter 9: Gentleness

1. Arthur Bennett, ed. *Valley of Vision: A Collection of Puritan Prayers* (Edinburgh: Banner of Truth, 2007), 1.

2. Dane Ortlund, *Gentle and Lowly: The Heart of Christ for Sinners and Sufferers* (Wheaton: Crossway, 2020), 18.

3. Christopher J. H. Wright, *Cultivating the Fruit of the Spirit: Growing in Christlikeness* (Downers Grove, IL: IVP, 2017), 127.

Chapter 10: Self-Control

1. Civilla D. Martin, "His Eye Is on the Sparrow," copyright 1905, public domain.

2. John Chrysostom, *Homilies of St. John Chrysostom on the Gospel according to Matthew,* ed. Philip Schaff, G. Prevost, and M. B. Riddle (trans.) (New York: Christian Literature Company, 1888), 10:228.

3. Abraham Kuyper, "Sphere Sovereignty" in *Abraham Kuyper: A Centennial Reader,* ed. James Bratt (Grand Rapids: Eerdmans, 1998), 461.

Conclusion

1. Neil Postman, *Amusing Ourselves to Death: Public Discourse in the Age of Show Business* (New York: Penguin Books, 2006), 155.

Appendix

1. John Webster, "Biblical Reasoning" in *The Domain of the Word: Scripture and Theological Reason* (London: T&T Clark, 2014), 115.

Scripture Index